TABOO

LIVING OUT

Gay and Lesbian Autobiographies

JOAN LARKIN AND DAVID BERGMAN, *General Editors*

Midlife Queer: Autobiography of a Decade, 1971–1981
Martin Duberman

Widescreen Dreams: Growing Up Gay at the Movies
Patrick E. Horrigan

Eminent Maricones: Arenas, Lorca, Puig, and Me
Jaime Manrique

Taboo
Boyer Rickel

TABOO
Boyer Rickel

THE UNIVERSITY OF WISCONSIN PRESS

The University of Wisconsin Press
2537 Daniels Street
Madison, Wisconsin 53718

3 Henrietta Street
London WC2E 8LU, England

5   4   3   2   1

Printed in the United States of America

Library of Congress Cataloging-in-Publication Data
Rickel, Boyer.
    Taboo / Boyer Rickel.
    144pp.   cm. — (Living out)
    ISBN 0-299-16260-5 (cloth : alk. paper)
    1. Rickel, Boyer.   2. Poets, American—20th century—Biography.   3. Gay men—
United States—Biography.   I. Title.   II. Series.
    PS3568.I35335Z47   1999
    811'.54—dc21   98-49498
    [b]

For my mother, Louise Rickel

Contents

ONE

Manhood

1

My earliest memory is of dustballs floating like ghosts along a brown, cracked, concrete floor . . . the flash of brass, a doorknob, as I fall . . . and Sen-Sen in a red and black paper package on the third level of the bookshelf beside my parents' bed . . . Sen-Sen, the smell of utter freshness, herbal and sweet . . .

. . . the smell of Tone, poking storefront to storefront along Tucson's Fourth Avenue, a downtown strip of thrifts and secondhand shops, three days before Halloween, 1979.

I followed as unobtrusively as I could. At first I wasn't sure if Tone was a he or a she. He wore black tights and green sandals, a coarse purplish shawl wrapped around his shoulders. The shawl tails hung down in front, draping the crotch. I inhaled everything, the spiked blond hair and dangling silver teardrop earrings. The round smooth face and large green eyes with smears of silver eyeshadow, a purple stripe above each eyelash. I guessed a he from the tiny ass and slightly muscular thighs.

Tone, who told me that afternoon, as we sipped coffee at a sidewalk cafe, that he was born in Boston to a Swedish au pair and the horny bisexual son of the Irish family she worked for. His father, a merchant marine, was still randy, Tone whispered with a wink. He rested his hand on my thigh, the shawl sliding down to expose a milk-white shoulder; six silver bracelets clacked to a halt against my

3

jeans. He was a jeweler, he said. He hoped to create perfumes some-day, and their bottles, of silver, for a few exclusive clients.

We walked three quick blocks to my apartment. Tone sat, legs extended across the couch, like Elizabeth Taylor in *Cleopatra*. This allowed the shawl to part, the sheer tights so form-fitting I could see distinctly his circumcision line. He talked about his well-connected friends in New York fashion circles and the stores, Berg-dorf's and Bloomie's, that would soon feature his jewelry. I started to tell him about the motel where I was desk clerk. I hoped to im-press him with stories of the hookers, or the bigots off the freeway on their way to California who often asked me if we had a "nigger problem" out west.

"I like the shape this little part makes here," he said, inter-rupting. He ran his finger down the middle of the lump made by his balls.

"I made a silver bolo tie for my last boyfriend using a clay-cast mold from the area right around here." Tone slid his tights down to his knees and, pulling his cock up toward his belly with one hand, traced a silver-dollar-size circle along the underside of his scrotum with a finger of the other. I could picture the bolo or-nament, two wrinkled lobes, like silver walnut shells. He talked on about things I didn't have the concentration to comprehend, cradling his balls and stroking his lengthening cock, gazing into my eyes as though disconnected from the manipulations.

He stopped talking when I pulled off my jeans. I lay down along his legs, kissing downward from his navel, intoxicated by the clean, sweet smell of Sen-Sen.

⌒

One tiny chip placed on the tongue released throughout the mouth a flavor that nearly stung with intensity. As a child I wasn't sure I liked it, not for itself; but I did like it because it seemed an almost forbidden pleasure, doled out ceremonially one or two chips at a time.

My father deliberately placed the package on a bookshelf too high for me to reach, beside the bed he shared with my mother. When I was four, I fell trying to climb the shelves. I huddled on the floor, determined not to cry out. It was then I noticed, floating under the bed, the dust ghosts, erratic phantoms darting suddenly or rolling purposefully along the concrete floor. They frightened me at first, but I was transfixed, distracted from my throbbing hip. I lay flat on the floor, pressing my belly into the coolness, and watched the movements of these apparitional beings.

I awoke at the touch of my father's hands. He lifted me gently, cradling me on his lap as he sat on the edge of the bed. Groggy, I couldn't fully figure where I was; he offered me Sen-Sen.

2

My father I see, papery ears fanning out from his head, brown hair slicked straight back, a slight slouch to his shoulders from years at the piano keyboard. He wears baggy, creased slacks, brown or gray, which I find beautiful because they shine, and short-sleeve buttoned-collar shirts, plain or printed in pale colors, always of the thinnest fabric, like the new slick fifties synthetics, so that the lines made by the straps of his undershirt show through. The single shirt pocket is stuffed with small white sheets of paper clipped together, his lists, which he checks throughout the day, crossing off accomplished tasks. At night the collection is reviewed and left with his keys and wallet and change purse on top of his dresser.

My father I see; my mother is nearly invisible, a ghost.

Is it possible to not actually be yourself at some point in your life? Could I have been so much my mother that I could not as a child see her any more than I could see myself, except by examining my image in the mirror?

My mother in the 1950s I gather in parts from photographs. From a snapshot of my brother's eighth birthday, her legs, thin and straight but strong with enough calf to give them shape, as she leans to cut the cake. A narrow waist, brown hair falling straight from the crown into a wave running ear to ear above her neck. From photos taken on desert picnics or during Sunday dinners at my grandmother's or at the piano in our living room where my mother gives private lessons to children, I see her skirts, some made of gingham, one red, another yellow, and one tan squaw dress with dozens of tiny pleats spoking downward from the belt, three concentric rows of metallic rickrack several inches from the hem.

In some memories of my first few years, my visual vantage is from high up looking down, as though I am carried by my mother, perched like a video camera at her shoulder. From this perspective I see my older brother in a homemade Indian outfit, a strip of terrycloth rag tied around his forehead for a headband with a pigeon feather standing up in back, red lipstick stripes on his cheeks, naked except for his underwear and a loincloth—two hand towels, one in front and one in back, draped on a belt.

Or we sit on the living room floor, my mother's books—she's taking an evening course in Greek mythology—scattered around us. I'm intrigued by nakedness, Achilles, Hermes, Aphrodite, in photographs of statues and painted urns in the various texts. While she reads and underlines and takes careful notes on small white cards, I draw with crayons the naked people from the books, or fingerpaint them on butcher paper, or, if she'll help me get set up, spread newspapers and sculpt in clay their whole forms, taking special care with the breasts and penises. And when I think it might be okay to interrupt, I ask her to tell me their stories.

In all these memories, she is a presence, a feeling, a warmth, even a voice, but not a physical body I can see. And so to know my mother in her young adulthood, I study my favorite photograph of her, taken some years before I was born. Behind her rise jagged mountains, the range just north of her college town. She sits atop a horse, which is pictured full-length facing left. She wears jeans, a fringed leather jacket, and a dark Stetson; she smiles toward the camera, her right hand on the horse's mane, her left holding the reins a few inches above the animal's neck.

To invent her eyes, her smooth skin, her youthful demeanor, I stare at this photograph. And from it I can ask her to step down and crouch beside the tan enamel tub, dark brown tiles extending from its edge up four feet on three sides, the bathtub of my childhood. I can ask her to rub my five-year-old's back with a soapy washcloth, and to sing a song with me. I love the crackly blueness of her eyes. I love the sweetness of her narrow lips, which have, by this time late in the day, only light traces of red lipstick on them.

This is the mother who encourages everything I try: small cakes from a mix in the child's oven on the back porch, an actual electric oven I stand before in one of her aprons dragging on the concrete pad; marriage to Cindy, the new girl across the alley with hair darker than my mother's; the mother who loans me scissors to cut my own hair before the ceremony, which I do without a mirror, trimming only the middle, down and down until I make a hole exposing my scalp; who helps me write braille letters to my father's blind sister, letters I compose by improvising the way I do when I dance in squaw dresses, according to the emotion of my thoughts, punching the stylus erratically into the special heavy paper, each letter a series of bumps bunched into dense colonies or oddly shaped groups or solitaries spread across the paper's smooth surface.

Not until my mother divorces my father when I am ten, not until we make up the beds with clean white sheets on the weekend, tucking opposite corners as I talk about the hollowness in my body from my father's absence, not till then does she take on a face and body I know I remember. More serious, her forehead slightly lined, the skin's pores now visible, her hair teased into a bubble and dyed a pale honey color, a result of the new luxury of weekly beauty parlor appointments in our town's only shopping center, she says, "Yes, I have that feeling too. I suppose we'll have it for a long time."

3

The sound of the same musical phrases played again and again, our house filled as always with a funereal presence the week before my father's piano recital, as though a body lay in state somewhere out of sight—I know this unsettled me. I was without doubt an annoyingly oversensitive child. My sister, eight years my senior, sat calmly through recitals like a little adult; my brother, the middle child, slept through performances. Before my feet could touch the floor, I perched on the edge of my seat, alert for the few—and inevitable—accidental notes my father would strike, each wrong note producing in me a sudden jolt of shame.

A pianist on the music faculty of Arizona State College, my father was not short-tempered. But at these times he was so taken up by the music, his concentration became palpable, a formidable presence; energy from normal household activities seemed somehow drained away into him, every conversation, every meal under a peculiar control—a control emanating, mysteriously, from him. I remember my mother and sister as virtually silent for days at a time. After meals, they'd wash dishes at the kitchen sink without speaking, both gazing out the window along separate lines.

I remember also, at this time in my life, my curiosity about the limits of things that were delicate, breakable—like our canary, such a small live creature. Once I deliberately clamped my teeth on a thermometer, gradually applying more pressure, frightened it would break—and delighted when it did, the mercury and slivers of glass on my tongue not lethal after all. How hard could I shake the cage, I wondered, before the bird stopped singing? If I knocked him down, would he hop up on the perch, a small wooden dowel, and sing again?

In the living room, beside my father's Steinway grand, stood the five-foot, shiny chrome bird-stand, shaped like a question mark. When my father practiced, experimenting with dynamic and rhythmic relationships of notes and phrases, repeating short passages over and over—to give each, as he explained, a spontaneous shape, a sculptural quality and life of its own—the canary sat silent in its cage, seemingly entranced by the singing of the piano, such an enormous, dark animal. But in a quiet house, mornings before even my mother had gotten out of bed, or evenings as we sat reading in the living room, the bird sang a pure high song that gave my father a particular pleasure. He'd reach over from his chair to my mother on the couch and touch her shoulder. "Just listen," he'd say, "how beautiful," in the voice he used to call us to the backyard patio on nights when the sky blazed orange and red at sunset. I'm sure there were even tears in his eyes, as there are occasionally tears in mine on such evenings now. Back then it was all my siblings and I could do to keep ourselves from laughing right out loud at his emotion. We held it in as best we could, but it sometimes drove us crazy to be called away to witness this incomprehensible grown-up rapture.

Shortly before I turned seven in the spring of 1958, the week of my father's recital, after several weeks of tense household restraint, my father at the college, my brother and sister at school, my mother hanging clothes in the back yard, I was left alone with the canary, who sang in full voice in the living room. I wrapped my fingers around the bird-stand and shook it until the bird slammed against the side of the wire cage, falling lifeless on the seeds and newsprint lining the birdcage floor.

I lied, hopelessly, when my father came home, as I had lied

not long before when he'd found his father's heirloom pocket watch no longer ticking atop his dresser. (Told never to put a magnet near the silver watchcase, I tried it the first chance I got.) The cage had obviously been shaken, all its furniture in disarray—perch and water bottle and mirror and green plastic seed dish toppled every which way.

I began to cry, and ran to my room. My father carried his beloved canary, Chipper, out the kitchen door to bury him.

I closed my door, curled up on my bed, and searched for the small manufacturer's tag on the pillowcase. I cultivated a smell in the area of this tag. I'd let saliva collect there as I sucked my thumb, until the spot took on a sweet bodily fragrance I associated with comfort and safety, my childhood narcotic. Whenever I was upset, I could lay my head on the pillow, inhaling this special fragrance, and fall into a deep, untroubled sleep.

4

How Did It All Start?
an essay by Dianne Rickel
for Mrs. White's fifth-grade class

We Rickel children were trying to decide what to be on Halloween. Always the first place to look is in the old trunk in the boys' bedroom. We found a ghost costume and a fairy costume and a Hawaiian grass skirt and many old clothes. Richard who was six decided on a ghost costume. It was black with white bones. I who was ten decided on an old beggar costume made from old Levi's and shirt. Boyer who was two called the fairy costume his "hula." Boyer thought the "hula" costume was very pretty so he decided that he would wear it.

At Halloween Boyer, you remember, wore his "hula" and also he wore earrings, lipstick, rouge, scarf, and green slipper socks. Every-

body thought he was a big sport to look like a girl when he was a boy. So day after day and week after week and month after month he wore his "hula" until we had to throw it out because it was too filthy. (Of course he didn't know where it went.)

Boyer was so unhappy that he could not find the "hula" so I let him wear my squaw skirt. So this went on day after day and week after week and month after month until we had to throw it away.

We decided to try hard to get him over this. Daddy bought him new Levi's and shirts. Some of Mother's girl pupils wore Levi's to lessons.

Mother wore her Levi's to teach in. Mrs. Wilber brought two of David's shirts. This idea worked part of the time. He insisted on wearing a dress especially when he saw someone in a dress. He was worse when there was a party.

Now with the squaw skirt gone he took to my lavender dress. To keep it clean Mother had to wash it sometimes twice a day. One day Mother did not have time to wash it and so we told him that Mother would wash it "tomorrow" and THIS went on day after day week after week and month after month.

On Mother's Day we had Grama Susie and the Brimhalls for dinner. When he saw us all dress up he remembered his dress and so he went out to the garage and into the dirty clothes to get his dress. He put it on by himself and came in to show it to us.

Day after day week after week month after month and year after year he wants to be a girl.

The End

5

For my flattop haircut, I went with my father, every two or three months, to Ray's Barbershop. A low, narrow structure, Ray's was just down from the newspaper office on the main commercial street and marked by a revolving barber pole, the red stripe spinning forever down or up, I couldn't decide. At age five and six, propped on a smooth board laid across the arms of the barber chair, a white smock fanning out from my neck, I'd fuss—I hated the buzzing clippers and being confined—till some treat, usually a piece of Dentyne gum, could be found to pacify me.

Entering Ray's, to the right one saw three black leather swivel chairs that rose and turned on pedestals like carnival rides; to the left, against the wall, a line of five or six green Naugahyde-covered chairs with chrome tube armrests. These waiting chairs I loved because their surfaces stung with coolness the skin on my arms and bare legs in the many hot months of the year. Having used up the cool of one spot, I'd lift my legs and shift my arms to a new position—enjoying even the unsticking sound—and use up the cool in the new location.

Despite the chairs, each time we neared Ray's those first few years, my fingers wrapped in my father's hand, I felt an odd sense of dread. Ray's was a world of men, men without women. If a mother had the job of seeing to her son's haircut, she'd usher him through the door, ask Ray to keep an eye out till she got some other errand done, and be on her way. This charged the atmosphere in some way that made me uncomfortable. Though the talk was generally good-natured, it took on the quality of a public competition, voices chiming in from all parts of the room, the volume rising and falling and rising again quickly.

And the talk seemed to follow a pattern. Whether a man agreed or disagreed with what had just been said—"What a lousy baseball team the college has this year" or "We need to pass those road bonds"—he'd have to up the ante, speaking more loudly, making a point, or countering a point, with greater intensity. A break in the buildup and he was out.

What made me most uneasy, though, was how my father, stepping through Ray's door, became someone else; how he suddenly treated me as an other, to be discussed as if not present, located in the third person: "I hope he's not too much trouble today, Ray." My father's voice would dip to a lower register, sounding flat and less gentle.

"A bad time to be in the stock market, Ray?" he'd ask, settling into the barber chair. I could see his shoulders, even beneath the smock, flatten against the chair-back—my father, who was otherwise noticeably round-shouldered. I could see that rather than take part in the actual contest, my father asked questions, deferring somewhat to the others. I was puzzled by the changes that took place in him; I was embarrassed by his awkwardness.

Some years later, as a member of the high school tennis team, I'd stand with about a dozen naked boys every day after practice in the open showers, the air thick with steam and the stink of gym clothes.

—"What a fuck-up Jimmy was in his match Thursday."

—"It'd serve that asshole right if Sally didn't let him touch her for a month."

—"Hey, Jimmy, she let you do stuff to her with that little wang of yours?"

Though we made our points with quick insults and sarcasm, the pattern was the same as in Ray's, each comment an attempt to top the one before.

Without calling too much attention to myself, I discovered how to add in a sentence here and there, not unlike my father's practice of posing questions. I'd snort at the appropriate moments, and find safe places (the splintered foot of an old wooden bench, a pile of discarded towels) to direct my gaze—away, always, from what interested and confused me most: the other boys' bodies.

⁓

By age twelve I visited Ray's alone, riding my bike downtown after school or on Saturday. Not only had I begun to figure out what made me uncomfortable there, I was becoming a student of character, intrigued by the manners of speech and dress and movement that gave adults their distinctive places in my small universe. Ray's was no good for this, the cast changing too quickly for long observation. But just a few blocks up and across the street, I found in another men's place, The Q, a pool hall, a cast of characters who daily arrived to take up their roles. Allowed, perhaps encouraged, to watch—these men knew how to play to an audience—I'd rent a table for half an hour, then sit with a cherry Coke at a distance to observe the drama.

The Q was cavernous, a huge open rectangle with lights like giant plungers hanging down over the green-felt-covered tables. Entering through the heavy glass door at one end of the storefront, you were met by a squinty little man with stringy dark hair and a stringy body, a body dried and smoked like beef jerky, and a few fading tattoos on his forearms. He sat behind a register near the door, at the end of a long snack counter. From any of the high stools along this counter one could turn and watch the nearby tables. The real action, though, was usually at a back corner snooker table, where the older characters—the Mex, Doc, Walter—would mix it up with the younger hustlers like Smitty, the Rail, and my brother, Richard.

Richard, four years my senior and in high school already, was friends with Smitty and the others; he could hold his own at this table. Always voluble, and tall, with a broad smile and crisp flattop haircut like mine, he could smoke and curse and talk about sex in conspiratorial ways with the other guys, hinting at conquests, winking, cigarette jittering between his lips, breaking into a growling laugh. All this carried off as he sighted along his cue to make a shot. Between turns he sat with three or four others in high plastic scooped chairs along the wall. They'd slouch in their seats, sticks standing straight up and held with both hands between their legs, comments floating side to side, heads rolling back and forth along the cool painted cinder block.

I was his kid brother, okay as long as he said so; he said so as long as I never made a point of being his brother. For hours I'd lurk outside the circle, witness to the give-and-take of men—from late adolescents like my brother, through the older unemployed or retired ones, some of them drunks, noses red and porous from years on the bottle.

Walter and the Mex were the lords of this latter group. Though Walter was light and the Mex dark, their bodies matched in almost every other way, paunches overlapping their belts, skin puffy yet creased here and there, brown eyes bloodshot as if they never slept. And their voices were ragged. Walter barked out phrases in hoarse bursts, tugging at his pants from the belt loops to emphasize a point. The Mex, quieter, was more inclined to ribbing Walter and the others than telling whole stories. "Better pull hard, my friend," he'd wheeze, "you got no ass to hold those pants up." They always looked and acted so settled, small grins and chuckles punctuating their remarks, I figured they had some secret to life.

The younger men handled themselves differently. If the rumpled Walter approached the snooker table like a respectful lover, deliberately considering each shot, gently placing the bridge-hand on the felt, his elbow coming to rest in one slow graceful motion, the young ones said with their bodies they would dominate. Volatile, loud, with quick eyes that knifed in anger or pleasure, Smitty charged the table, swiftly finding the desired angle, pulling the cue back in precise but sudden preliminary jerks. Missing an important shot, Rail, nicknamed for both his skill with bank shots and his skinny frame, would slam the butt of his cue against a wall, spitting a curse. And there were actual fights—over debts (these games were played for money), over occasional insults (about little peckers and never getting laid, or somebody's dumpy girlfriend). Sometimes I couldn't see the explosion coming. There'd be the thud of bodies against a table, arms and grunts and teeth in a blur, and then five or six men rushing in to pull the bodies apart. Those of us just

Manhood

15

watching would scatter to the walls like so many water droplets shaken from a rag.

I was scared almost to trembling each time I walked into The Q—and excited by my fear. But it wasn't because of the fights. It had to do with my role as a watcher. I felt no kinship with either group, the fiery young hustlers or their blowsy elders, though both I found fascinating. I knew I was a spy, an imposter. I was terrified some comment or some stupid stumbling gesture would show them who and what I was. And though I didn't know what that would be, I felt certain something fundamental in my nature would be different, and to these men, to my brother, even, unacceptable. So I held myself in absolute, nearly frozen, reserve. If I was blank, I thought, if I didn't try to show I was anybody, if I simply watched, smiled, smirked, laughed at the right moments, slouched down in my chair, I'd pass.

6

We talked about Mozart, we talked about rock and roll, the Beatles, the Doors, about sports, about teachers we knew in common at the high school. We took turns at the piano. I played simple pieces by Purcell and Bach and Handel; he knew jazz and swing, inventing looping passages of darkness and humor. He showed me his watercolors, wondrous, dense worlds of vegetation, vine and tree and flower, with animals. He was two years younger, a freshman, my best friend Will's little brother. Brown as earth, his eyes nearly black, short and lean with luminous skin.

We'd lie on the living room floor, propped on our elbows, shoulder to shoulder, looking over a piano score. We'd shoot baskets at the hoop over his garage door; I'd tease by wrapping my arms around him from behind, to keep him from driving for a lay-up. I sensed something in him, like a secret, some vitality, that spilled into me whenever I was near him.

Whereas I arranged my bedroom in precise order—bed tightly made, dresser drawers aligned, desk a geometry of books and pens and stapler—Leon's was in a disarray suggesting, I realized instantly, *life:* albums and clothes and a broken, overturned fish tank and a blond imitation-wood fifties Zenith TV the size of a hay bale and, of course, an unmade bed with baseball cards and marbles and notebook pages crumpled and tossed among the sheets. And the walls were plastered with pencil drawings and paintings and maps and magazine ads for guitars and posters of rock stars. He'd even put large hooks on one wall from which he hung jackets and a camera and a Boy Scout canteen. You almost had to kick your way through the clutter, scooping away a spot on the bed to sit. I could have burrowed in the profusion of that room; I could have shouted for the joy of such energy. I managed on my second visit to make off with a threadbare, soiled, plain brown T-shirt, which I hid in my closet and slept with for weeks, my dreams incoherent and sensual and redolent of Leon.

The wind had a bitter edge I'd not expected. We dug a shallow pit the size of a small backyard swimming pool in the sand. Five of us— Leon, his best friend, Tom, Will, another mutual friend, and I—all tumbled in. Woozy from a night of drinking, we pulled sleeping bags around ourselves, squirming into comfortable spots. The wind would swell, the sound filling my ears, before I'd realize it was the ocean, the breaking of a wave creeping up the shore. I lay next to Leon. This was my second trip to the Gulf of California, a spot not far from the U.S. border where Leon's family camped often. It was Thanksgiving of 1967.

We'd been carousing in town at several cantinas. Mixing with other American kids, set free to drink in public, we shouted the lyrics to songs we knew on the jukeboxes, pissed in the dimly lit dirt streets, tried to hit on the few American girls who could shake their parents.

I'd felt some physical charge, some urgency this night, as strong from Leon as emanated from me. I felt it now as we lay on the beach, my mind growing powerfully clear, a sense of inner focus opening up inside me. I could actually visualize the aura encircling me and Leon, whose eyes were—I knew without looking—also open to the night sky. And then one by one, inexplicably, the other boys hauled their sleeping bags out of the pit.

I stared at the stars. *Dense as spilled powder,* I thought, *we* thought, the thought not mine but *ours,* my whole body now infused with Leonness. We turned to look at each other and exchanged an inner howl of recognition and fear and then the absolute joy of the amazing telepathy. Was this God?

I lay in a state of exhilaration—and absolute tension, possessed by Leon, Leon by me. I'd never felt so vital, our bodies two parallel, blended, sensual vessels. I longed to embrace him. Yet we agreed, silently, that we shouldn't touch. Like the sound of our own voices, surely touching would break the spell. And so it went through the night, during which we lay side by side, perfectly still, and spoke not once, but thought together, using not words exactly and not imagery—pure thought, as energy, as spirit. *So this is what it means to be alive.*

First morning light was a millennium arriving, arriving in a no-time, in a second. We rose and laughed, our first sounds in hours. The rest of the day we had a power over and *in* each other, a connection that we'd test. That night, across a crowded cantina, a swirl of drunk Americans, a few Mexicans, dancing and shouting, a few couples necking: I can see the haze and feel the sweat sticking my shirt to my skin as I talk excitedly to Will and my head gets pulled, my gaze forcibly drawn across the room to where Leon is staring into me.

We had this connection for weeks. And I was changed; we

were changed. We'd sit at the piano and improvise wildly for hours, the music itself a way of knowledge passing between us. We'd find tiny resonances of our new sense of life's possibility in a Charles Ives quartet, a Thelonious Monk piano riff, in paintings by Gauguin and van Gogh. We tried to express the mystery, Leon in paintings and a journal, I in poems and short, allegorical stories.

Over the months the intensity diminished; still that night in Mexico remained a powerful source. We could spark it to life especially at the piano, though I grew anxious over what seemed a draining of our intimacy.

One evening, over a year later, at a time when I was thinking more and more about college, my plans to enroll in a small midwestern liberal arts school, wondering what would happen to me and Leon, we attended a recital together. It was held at a private center for the performing arts in the desert north of town. The small adobe building reserved for chamber recitals had room for only three or four rows of chairs, arranged in a rectangle. In the middle was space for the performers. Concerts there, which I usually attended with my father, always seemed special. When the lights were turned down, one looked toward a circle of glowing musical scores lit by lamps clipped to the music stands, the musicians nodding in and out of the light as they performed.

On this night's program, before intermission, members of a German string sextet played two works, the first a quartet by Mozart, as delicate, as purely architectural as a spider's web. Then a monumental Brahms sextet, a piece that builds in its final movement from a brooding fugue toward six independent, translucent, ethereal threads, a journey on the breath of angels. I sat, as the house lights came up, transported somewhere beyond my self, astonished at the beauty and strangeness in being alive.

On a patio where intermission refreshments were being served, Leon asked me what I thought. Wanting to please him, to show myself in perpetual harmony with him, I lied—surely I'd heard him fidget during the Brahms? "I liked the Mozart best," I said. "The other went on too long."

"Oh no." His voice cracked with hurt.

Neither of us spoke again till we got back to town.

I can never think of that lie—a lie about a moment of near-spiritual significance—without feeling sick. I have no idea what was played after intermission. I spent the time composing apologies, some confession of what I'd done and why. But my shame confused me; it seemed too crazy to explain. I couldn't tell him I loved him, because I didn't know it myself.

7

I was forever forming secret alliances with other boys, clubs with codes and shifting hierarchies. We played war games, spied on neighbors, made up elaborate stories of how we'd someday rule the world. We'd meet in our older brothers' tree forts. These were perched in the cottonwoods—huge white-skinned trees with broad yellowish leaves—alongside canals that ran through our neighborhoods. From the top of such trees, we thought we could see the curve of the Earth.

Such secret places were also good for talking about sex and, whenever possible, looking at pornographic magazines. The college dorms were only blocks from our houses; by the time we were nine or ten, we knew that at each semester's end, the young college men, graduating or returning to their parents' homes, would have to throw out the pornography they'd collected over the term. We'd root through the garbage cans, clustered in small, three-sided, red-brick enclosures behind the dorms, whooping with glee when we discovered a cache of magazines, spiriting them to one of our hideouts.

And sex, of course, was a remarkably empowering secret. I can remember feeling somehow important, strong, for days at a time after a sexual experiment with a friend or a first long look at a new set of magazines; I walked with an inner confidence I knew the adults couldn't see from the outside, that I owned from within.

〜

Homo. The word was so dark and ugly I couldn't say it. *Nigger* one couldn't say because it hurt, it offended, its ugliness the power to injure; when spoken, it produced in my mind the image of a painful flesh wound. But *homo*'s ugliness grew out of the filth and degradation homos practiced, and the places they habituated.

Homos did it, boys were told by their older friends and brothers, under the abandoned, broken-down train bridge spanning the dry riverbed at the north end of town, not far from the public pool. The pool, with its small attached park, was located at the foot of a newer bridge for cars a quarter mile east of the old bridge. Through the 1950s and early sixties we had a family pass and swam at the pool all summer long. Parents could drop off their children for the day, knowing they'd be watched by the lifeguards.

But bums lived not far away, back of the oleanders at the edge of the park, under the old train bridge, their skin a grimy gray-brown. They reeked of urine, and worse, they were homos. When they ventured into town at night, they always hung out along the railroad tracks or in the dark areas of parks, doing what they did in the public restrooms.

During these same years, when I was between six and ten, there was nothing I loved more than having sex with friends. One boy in particular enjoyed taking turns with me, top and bottom, in the missionary position, rubbing our genitals together until it almost hurt—or, what seemed more common, until we were caught, our secret out, though I was gratified to discover how soon the adults, embarrassed and righteous, were willing to forget.

Once in second grade, after the midmorning recess bell had

rung to call us in, Tony, a chunky Hispanic, the class giant, with skin dark as potting soil and the broad face of a Navajo, pushed me to the floor of a restroom stall. We'd shared the toilet, peeing from either side. He latched the metal door, guiding me to lie face down. Then he lay on top of me, pushing and wiggling to get his penis in. It felt almost good, the warmth of his weight and the pressure, though the linoleum was sticky and cold.

"Now you try," he said, peeling me back with an oversized hand. As I got started, we began to slide, as if the earth had tilted under us. Angelo, the janitor, had grabbed Tony's ankles, which extended from under the stall. He dragged us into the center of the restroom.

Angelo said nothing. He never said anything. I'm not sure he spoke English. I was mortified, too shaken to pull my own pants up. Tony matter-of-factly buckled himself, then helped me to button my jeans, my underwear bunched uncomfortably around the bottoms of my butt cheeks, and pushed me out the door.

⁓

Age seven, when a neighbor boy taught me how to masturbate, the sensation of tugging the loose skin up and down around my small hard penis was purely thrilling in and of itself. I needed no image, no story, to bring me to a dry, electric climax.

In a few years, though I enjoyed having sex with other boys, the magazines provided new and provocative images when I was alone: large smooth breasts, nipples dark and textured like raspberries, and tight round buttocks. I'd slip into the bathroom I shared with my brother, a magazine hidden under my shirt. I'd sit on the toilet, slowly turning the pages, the photos sparking instant erections and quick ejaculations. There was sex talk among us boys about girls, how some at school showed signs of breasts; we speculated about which would let us kiss them on the lips.

By junior high, sex games with other boys were out of the

Manhood

22

question. Now we tested our manhood, which meant going as far as we could with girls. Boys who did things with other boys were homos, to be ridiculed, hardly male at all. Needled by a friend about how I used to like beating off with guys, I'd deny everything, my fury so righteous I almost believed my own words.

We dated, we necked at parties with girls, we began to learn the prevailing story of sex: the teasing and awkward conversations between classes, the meetings after school for Cokes and visits in the kitchen with the girl's mother, the wrestling out of sight of parents in the yard or on the living room carpet, the long phone calls and the notes passed between friends. When beating off at night in bed, I'd lie back on the pillow and close my eyes, imagining impossible circumstances—in her bedroom or mine, or at night in the park—the story's climax a literal one. Meanwhile, it was particular friends, boys, whose bodies sent complex feelings of pleasure through me.

Gradually, through high school, I began to move boys into my fantasies. In plot, these were no different from my stories about girls, equally impossible, equally thrilling—sex after school under the athletic field bleachers, sex in his bedroom, where we'd gone to do algebra homework. But what such fantasies might signify was literally unthinkable. I experienced this as forgetting: daily, automatic, painless. For all I knew, I was just like my friends, forever horny, forever hoping for the chance to go all the way with a pretty girl; settling, gladly, at parties and drive-ins for endless, tongue-filled kisses, the stroking and sucking of breasts, and the sweetness, on lucky nights, of delirious moans and mutual hand- and finger-powered orgasms.

By college all my sexual fantasies were homosexual, though their meaning was screened from my conscious mind. My eyes scanned classes, concert audiences, waiting lines in grocery stores, tables in the student union beer hall, for men, images of men to call up when I needed them, to live inside my narratives. The search was automatic, unconscious, as if performed by some other, some separate, intelligence. Otherwise, I behaved as did my new male college friends, acting out the rituals of romance we'd been practicing since junior high—pursuits, flirtations, seductions, long serious talks, short-term monogamies—with women.

In glacial increments, through the four college years, my conscious mind began to waken. Why did I beat off with men in my mind, then sleep with so many women? Could the feelings I had for men, my fantasies about them, belong to me? Might they be *my* story?

It delighted me to see men dance with men at parties. When I joined in, it didn't mean I was a homo. Age twelve, I shared my father's disgust as we turned the pages of a *Life* magazine photo layout of the Beatles: their hair edging over their ears, the pointy heels on their black zippered boots—were these guys or girls? But since high school in the late 1960s, my friends and I had questioned so many of our parents' codes. By 1968 I was on the principal's list of students called every few months from classes to check hair length: over the collar in back and we were out. We were nicknamed "the Dirty Thirty."

In college I pierced an ear and wore a dangling earring; I grew my hair to the middle of my back; I toted books and wallet and keys in an over-the-shoulder satchel much like a purse. Who knew where a new sense of maleness might lead? If out with a woman friend, I'd wait beside the car while she opened the door; at a formal restaurant, we'd enjoy the waiter's confusion as she ordered meals for both of us. I took a sexuality course with a girlfriend; we talked about the need to embrace the Other residing in each of us, her male self, my female self.

~

Once in high school, twice in college, I had girlfriends I cared for deeply, women I knew other young men in my position would have asked to marry. Something held me back; I couldn't name it. "I'm not feeling what I'm supposed to feel," I said to each in turn. I feared I couldn't love.

The week of college graduation, I slept with two close friends, both women, a consequence of all-night parties and a profound sense of freedom, of not quite being anyone I knew. We were all between selves, the old ones we had become these past four years and the new ones surfacing, based on the old, facing an unknowable future. Our sex was gentle and dreamy and without complication, a form of farewell. We showered after hours of dancing and drinking, made love, slept, made love, showered again, talcing each other's bodies against the stickiness of a midwestern May. In bed we took our time, rolling to change positions without letting go. We lay half the day among the sheets, giggly as children, emptied of responsibility—no papers due, no exams, and no need to discuss where our relationship was going. It was going nowhere.

That week I also slept with two men following parties, men I hardly knew. The first I'd noticed in the dining hall where we both worked. After dancing together, flirting openly, kissing a little, he took me to his dorm room under the pretext of listening to Mahler's "Kindertotenlieder." I'd loved this work for years in a recording by a mezzo-soprano. A voice major, this tall, green-eyed sophomore with sandy, thinning hair, wanted me to hear the songs interpreted by a man, a tenor, he said.

The sex was awkward, elbows in all the wrong places, my body too angular, too skinny, the prickle of mustaches as we necked a shock; my cock too meager, I feared, his much too grand for me to manage gracefully. This first time with a man, I had little idea of the mechanics, my beard stubble scratching the inside of his thighs, my teeth causing him to cry out, "Why do I get all the virgins!" He laughed as he lifted my head from his crotch.

I was grateful for his humor, his ease, his patience. I inhaled in gulps the fragrances of his body, the muskiness gathered in the hourglass-shaped mat of hair at the center of his chest, the pungency in the seam between his inner thigh and scrotum.

At two A.M., I walked to the house I shared with friends, delirious with recognition, feeling tall as a giant; the sidewalk seemed miles down to my feet. I had glimpsed what I had missed, what I had been unable to feel, with women.

While having sex, though intensely anxious, my voice trembling and my tongue chalk-dry, I'd been released, paradoxically, from the burden of self-consciousness: I felt like myself.

TWO

Man Shrinking

I discovered one afternoon in 1963, two years after my parents' divorce, that a man could shrink. That night my father lay on his side in bed, snoring so loudly it did no good for me to sleep in the living room, a closed door between us, with a pillow over my head. The terrible human ripping sounds, the bellowing gurgles and choking gasps, penetrated walls and doors with ease. It did no good, even, to drag my blankets onto the front porch. I sat curled in a heap on the concrete slab, my back to the door, a sheet wrapped around my shoulders, to await sunrise. At one point, standing in the damp grass, I actually placed my hand on the glass of my father's bedroom window to see if it didn't vibrate.

It was Saturday night in a section of town given over to apartments for college students, young married couples, and bachelors. I counted each car slowing to a stop—someone home late from a party or bar, footsteps along one of the eight parallel curb-to-front-door concrete sidewalks on the block, the slap of a front-door screen—I counted each of these faceless human diversions from my sleeplessness a blessing, a tiny story to break up the monotony. And off and on, I considered the new possibility of a man shrinking.

My father's one-bedroom apartment was within walking distance of the college music building where he taught piano. One side of a duplex, it had tan linoleum tile floors and speckled tan tile on the kitchen and bathroom counters, which I'd scrub each Saturday as I cleaned the place—my visits a means, I understand now, of maintaining our domestic connection following the divorce.

Though utterly ordinary, much about the ritual remains vivid: beside his bed and bathroom sink the lacquered reed wastebaskets that I emptied, the swirl of pinks in the low marble coffee table that I dusted, and the gray German reel-to-reel we'd set between the couch and reading chair so we could listen after lunch to music from his extensive collection of tapes. Lunch was usually something simple that I could prepare—crackers with sliced apples, bananas, and cheese, or tuna sandwiches with glasses of milk. I enjoyed arranging our portions on the plates, as well as the plates and glasses and silverware on the table, in patterns that were pleasing.

This particular Saturday, as on several others, he placed, every four hours, a tiny green tablet under his tongue to ease the pain of a migraine. And in the afternoon, while I read in the living room, he lay down to rest.

He called me into his room after only an hour, oddly buoyant in his pale blue boxers and white undershirt, hair flattened on one side of his head. Stretching out full-length, he insisted I measure him, right there on the bed, head to foot. Four years from my own driver's license, I'd studied his often, the deadening photograph and official numbers and seals the true ticket, I thought, to adulthood. Under height his read 5'11". I knew this and the other bits of information—middle name (Pooler), birthdate (5/3/14), and so forth—by heart. So when the tape came to sixty-nine inches, only five-foot-nine, I suggested he get out of bed and stand next to a wall.

"I must be shrinking," he said. "It happens to men as they get older." (He was only forty-nine.) "My father was once almost six feet tall."

I couldn't believe it, not about my diminutive Gramps, who, when he barbecued, like a sweet, bald, leathered girl, enjoyed, after one too many Schlitz beers, raising the hem of his white apron to perform a little can-can. The Gramps I knew, with hunched shoulders and drooping eyelids, couldn't be much above five-foot-six now.

Growing in bursts, all legs, knobbed knees, and lank, unretract-

Man Shrinking

able arms, I found this possibility, that a man could shrink, more than unsettling; I was for a few days close to paralyzed mentally, obsessed with the thought that my father from here on in would become less and less, that someday this would happen to me.

～

Nearly thirty years have passed since those Saturdays I spent with my father in his bachelor apartment. Remarried shortly before I entered college, he suffered a stroke a year later, in 1970. Through intensive therapy and the dedication of his new wife, he appeared to recover almost completely. His voice, after several weeks of stumbling over common words, grew full and confident again. He continued his teaching and maintained his usual activities, though he no longer gave recitals. Only in his bearing, a leaning to the left to compensate for weakened muscles along that side, a bias that increased by increments over the years, could you see the stroke's effects.

Then in 1989, age seventy-five, he took a fall on a walk in the neighborhood; and then he took another some months later, in his home, when my stepmother was away for the afternoon. Though he broke no bones, he lay on his side, trapped by the weight of the weaker left leg atop the right, unable even to crawl to a phone. In the months that followed, he grew more frail, moving from a hardwood cane to an aluminum-frame walker. At present, wheelchair-bound, he must be attended much of the time. No longer able to stand on his own, he wears a small emergency button on a chain around his neck in case he slips out of the wheelchair or out of bed when he's alone.

And so it was that I drove two hours one recent Saturday morning—from my home in Tucson to Tempe—to care for my father, to spend the day with him; this would enable Carol, my

stepmother, to leave their house at dawn for a hike in the Super-
stition Mountains near Phoenix.

Upon my arrival, but before unlocking the door off their covered driveway, I reviewed Carol's written instructions—a step-by-
step explanation of how to get my father from bed to shower, how
to bathe and then dress him, how to prepare his ritual breakfast. I
was determined to remember what needed to be done; the idea of
consulting her notes in front of him struck me as vaguely shameful,
as though taking care of my father were something like following a
recipe.

He lay on his side, facing the door, eyes like tiny lights in the
darkened room as I entered. "So how's my boy," he said, toothless,
through sunken lips. (Getting his teeth in would be one of our first
priorities.)

I have spent the last several months puzzling over the power
of those few words: "So how's my boy." After hearing them, I felt
changed, changed into someone I had not been for a very long
time. Much about the day that had worried me—bathing my father,
for example—became simplified.

My father's full height is now about four feet. He's so
stooped, so utterly curled over on himself, that when he stands,
grasping someone's arm or a walker for support, he must cock his
head painfully to one side like a bird to speak to other standing
adults.

But there was no strangeness in stripping down together, in
guiding him by the arm into the special shower; no strangeness in
running the cloth, soggy with soap, through the ripples of his flesh,
his breasts hanging down over his chest; no strangeness in soaping
his penis and scrotum and the crack of his ass as he gripped the
metal wall-bars for balance. It was not like bathing a baby; it was
not another example of an often-noted irony—the parent becoming
the child, the child the parent.

He had called me in a special way with those words, rising

from his curled form the moment I walked through the bedroom door; he had called me by an earlier name, a child-name—the one who took pleasure serving.

After the bath, after rubbing lotion on his legs and hips, helping him slip on socks and sweats and a pale blue polo shirt, and then dressing myself, I made breakfast for us, boiling water for coffee, quartering cantaloupe, while he explained from his wheelchair exactly how he wanted each item prepared: half a cup of skim milk stirred four or five times into the steaming instant oatmeal, and orange juice just to the point he noted with his left index finger, two inches from the rim. It was all a pleasure, this getting things right. Being the son had not been for almost thirty years so unthreatening.

For me and many of my middle-aged friends, parents calling our child-names, or those names rising up within us spontaneously, is one of the complications of returning to our childhood homes. We spend half our lives, it seems, getting our parents to honor our adult selves—an effort running parallel to the long process of our coming to believe those selves do in fact exist. Bristling when they attempt to help in our decisions, we ask ourselves in secret: But when do I grow up? When do I take command in the way my parents did when I was a kid? (Increasingly, I've come to wonder if my parents' self-possession wasn't simply a child's fantasy, fulfilling my need for security.)

Since leaving home for college, how many Christmas dinners at my mother's have I thought I heard the impossible opposition of my child and adult names being used simultaneously. Year after year, as we slice the tomatoes, break lettuce for the salad, decide on tablecloths and napkins and how to arrange the chairs, as we negotiate these simple tasks (negotiations I can undertake effortlessly with friends), my child and my adult seem to get all confused. I grow stupidly angry if told what to do or if a decision doesn't go my way. Who do you think I am? I want to demand. And then, to myself,

Who *am* I? To my mother, of course, how could I be anything but both child and adult—I am her child still, after all.

Following breakfast on this Saturday with my father, I rolled him from the kitchen to the living room. Having locked the wheels of his chair in place and nudged the footrests to the sides, he planted his feet on the carpet, gripped the armrests, and scooted forward on his rump to the seat's edge. Then, standing behind him, I lifted from the armpits as he used the strength in his legs and arms to push himself upward. Turning slowly to face me, he fell gently back, settling with a *humph* and a snort of laughter into the overstuffed reclining chair next to the couch.

Throughout the day we took turns listening and conversing, each of us having saved up something special to share with the other. I played the tape of my recent poetry reading, Dad concentrating on the photocopied texts of poems he held on his lap, smiling now and then, eyes narrowing, sometimes pursing his lips, eyebrows rising each time he licked his finger to turn a page. I didn't hear a word of the tape, I was so taken up by the changes in his face.

Late in the afternoon, shortly before my return drive to Tucson, he read me a new favorite essay he had found, a dazzling meditation by Lance Morrow on the meaning of home. In it, Morrow writes:

> *Creation is an onion with many skins all layering outward from the child's self. If he gets lost in the galaxy, he can find the way back, can fly through the concentric circles to his own house—from outermost remoteness to innermost home. Nostalgia means the* nostos algos, *the agony to return home.*

After a silent moment at the essay's conclusion, I asked him to please read it again—not to hear the words so much as to hold on to a new feeling, a feeling I could not at that moment name: beside the father, the child and son and man all in one.

Angel

"Mr. Man!" the children shriek, racing in a line, as orderly as ducks, down the dirt drive of the property next to ours. They're bare-chested, brown, all giggles and coated in dust. Five boys and a girl, Veronica. Crossing the street, they gather into a busy cluster, atoms bouncing off one another. We stand in a patch of dried Bermuda where Lucy, my white standard poodle, wags impatiently. Before us stretches our street's adoptive playground—a block-deep, gravel-covered vacant lot, bordered on either side by enormous warehouses.

The boys outshout each other to throw the ball: "First, first, I go first!" Angel, whose diaper half-hobbles him, stamps his feet. Veronica, shy, sucks a finger.

I drop the ball into Fabian's outstretched palm.

"Oooh," he shudders, launching it, "it's slobbery." Lucy leaps to snag it on a single bounce.

The boy next in line I don't recognize. The only one to wear an earring, a gold stud the size of a rattler's eye. His black hair's been buzzed Marine-style like the other boys'—except theirs, at the neckline, falls in a sheer cascade, a detail that never fails to delight me.

"How old's your dog?" he asks.

"Eight. How old are you? Did you just move in?"

"I'm nine," he says. "I'm visiting."

"You a friend of Fabian's from school?"

"Nah, he's my uncle."

This time I contain my surprise. One evening last week, I asked José to give a girl I took to be his baby sister a turn throwing the ball. He corrected me matter-of-factly: "Tina's not my sister, she's my aunt."

Until recently, children living next door tended to be a few years older than the current group—and toughened beyond routine hellos to the likes of us, two men in their forties. One boy, a thirteen-year-old, hacked arms from a thriving San Pedro cactus in our back yard. My partner, Gary, confronted his parents. The mother, an obese woman whose slurred, loud ramblings made us think her slightly retarded, bellowed for the boy to get in the house; the father, at least twenty years her senior, a scrap collector with a weathered, sunken face and a few stumps for chewing, promised to give the boy a good beating.

Within a few months, the boy and his parents moved out, replaced by another poor family. Which is how it goes with tenants of the five tiny ramshackle cottages next door. They're among the most run-down in our neighborhood, where houses, an irregular blend of bungalows, Victorians, and territorials, range from the boarded-up to *House and Garden* renovations. Tucked alongside downtown Tucson, we're a human blend as well, Anglo and Hispanic, many of us gay: artists and writers and teachers; people on welfare, some living in Section Eight housing; artsy college students; blue-collar families; and a fair number of homeless. Our street marks the neighborhood's eastern edge, right up against a warehouse district.

Now that school's out for the summer, now that our days routinely rise above one hundred degrees, the next-door children gather and disperse all over the block, independent and fearless as insects. The way I remember kids used to, the way Gary and I did in our Phoenix and Tempe neighborhoods in the 1950s. Were we youngsters today,

I can't imagine our parents giving us the run of the streets. They'd enroll us in day camps. We'd get swimming and art lessons or learn to use computers, as do our friends' children.

Sticks are our neighbor kids' most important toys, which they transform daily into guns, horses, swords, magic wands. I used to worry they'd poke out their eyes or otherwise impale each other. But the boys and girls alike wave them expertly as they race from yard to driveway to the vacant lots—the one across the street and another much smaller one bordering our back yard, where two giant tamarisks grow. One afternoon last week, the cicadas humming like transformers, I noticed a plastic orange warning flag wiggling high up among a tamarisk's branches. One of the boys had climbed up, perhaps as a lookout or spy in some war game. He'd probably snatched the flag from the water-line project down the block, a trench surrounded by blinking barricades. Not wanting to spoil his fun, I pretended not to see him.

I confess, though most of these kids have lived here for months, it wasn't till recently I warmed to them. Over the years, too many flowers ripped from our gardens, too much garbage—chicken bones, beer cans, old clothes, broken toys—thrown in our yard by people living in the rentals.

Gary can see the new arrivals as new arrivals; he always manages to hope for the best. I see them as part of one extended family that has caused us so much aggravation.

When kids move in, Gary invites them to help him plant the flower beds. If he sees them trailing African daisies down the sidewalk, he tells them it's okay to pick flowers, if they'll only ask. "We'll put together a bunch for your mother," he suggests. I'm inclined to holler from the porch, "Get out of our yard! I'm gonna tell your father!"

But Angel has changed me. More than once I gasped to see him toddling unattended across the street. I'd run next door, shouting, "Can somebody come get this baby?" Usually Fabian wandered out, in no particular hurry. His eyes spoke eloquently: *Take it easy, man, what's your problem?*

Then one evening a few weeks back, I was playing ball with Lucy just before nightfall. I'd tossed the ball several times, wondering if one of the kids would spot us and alert the others. I was starting to almost miss them when they didn't join us.

Out marched Angel, diapered and barefoot as usual. Snug to his chest he clutched a skateboard that was as tall as—and wider than—himself. He crossed the street, then the narrow parking lot sloping gently up to the warehouse.

Down he threw the board, heaving himself on, belly first, launching toward the street. I spotted a car coming and started yelling, "Angel! Angel!" as I ran toward him.

He ignored me, rolling to a stop right at the gutter as the car swept by. From his special vantage, he'd noticed what I hadn't, the pavement's last-second rise, a lifesaving change of a few degrees. Jumping up, he flashed me a smile. He swung the skateboard aloft, then balanced it on his head as he strode up the slope to do it again.

Soldiers

In the late fifties, my boyhood friends and I hid from Nazis. We lived in Tempe, Arizona, at that time a small farming and college town with a single, hooked main drag running south from the dry Salt River bed, which marked the community's northern edge. World War II little more than a decade past, swastikas and Nazi salutes fired our imaginations far more than the newer, less tangible Commies. When we played war, we looked for secret hiding places, the safest being in Grady Gammage Jr.'s home. With broad concrete steps up to a front porch enclosed with tall, narrow, multipaned windows, this dignified two-story house was unlike any other I knew, probably a Queen Anne or Anglo-territorial from the turn of the century. All my other friends lived in one-story ranch-style houses like ours.

Grady was the college president's son, the shortest boy in class, with fine black hair, parted on the side and greased to a lacquered shine, perfectly combed, as if painted on his head. I remember his face as always serious, the deep-set dark eyes and long thin nose producing angularities most people's faces take on later in adulthood. His house was the traditional President's Family Residence, at the heart of the Arizona State College campus. When I'd visit on Saturdays, an aging housekeeper whose accent made me think her German-born, and whom Grady called Gram, would fix us ham sandwiches with the crusts sliced off; she'd place these, with small cups of canned fruit and glasses of milk, on the tiny table-and-chair set in Grady's playroom. He had one whole room set aside for toys, and a substantial, carpenter-made tree house, right on the property, so unlike the rickety scrap-wood structures made by my older brother and his friends in the cottonwoods that stood alongside canals in town.

After lunch, Gram safely out of the way in the kitchen washing dishes, we'd tiptoe to the house's central staircase. In the wall along the upper level was what Grady called his secret door, behind which rose a set of steps, a passageway into complete darkness where we'd hide from the Nazi storm troopers.

Each time Grady led me to this door, I was thrilled by the secrecy and danger, by the enormity of what was at stake, life or death, which we comprehended only vaguely.

The passageway itself was so dark, no matter how long we waited for our pupils to adjust, we saw nothing but absolute black, a blackness that pressed up against our eyes. We'd touch the wall to steady ourselves as we walked a few steps up. Then we'd sit and whisper about whom we'd lock out and whom we'd invite to join us and thereby save. After several minutes of this, we'd creep back down and listen at the back of the door, making sure no one was on the stairs before slipping out.

~

Another game we played just once. We were now eight. I don't remember if it was a weekend or holiday, but I was home in the morning when a call came. Could someone bring Boyer to play with Grady? the caller asked. His father had died of a heart attack, and Grady would be spending the day at a house near ours.

I contemplated the gravity of this news, the first human death of my life, as I rode in the back of our car. I ran my hand over the seamed blue surface of the car seat, and tried to imagine life without my father or mother, a desperately painful fantasy. Grady met me at the front door. His eyes were not red from crying; his voice was steady. But I could tell he held himself in absolute reserve. Some invisible force maintained the expressions of his face, the modulations of his voice, in a middle, controlled register.

In my memory, the day unfolds without adults; no doubt I was so absorbed in my own thoughts, I failed to take notice. I don't recall who took the phone call, who drove, or why I sat alone in the back seat of the car instead of in front. I don't recall who, other than Grady, was at the house, a low, red-brick bungalow, or how Grady and I found our way to the back yard. There, both of us in a kind of trance, we played with small toy soldiers and did not talk about his father's death. We dislodged with trowels, and then lined up in two parallel columns diagonally at the center of the lawn, bricks that had circled, ornamentally, several tree-wells. Then we marched battalions of army men along the brick roads.

When we got to the roads' end the first time, I was at a loss. There was no purpose to this game. We didn't have a story to go with it. We were simply doing things mechanically to keep ourselves occupied. After a pause, Grady commanded, "March back." And so we did.

At home that evening, I lay down in the cool grass of our back yard, staring up at the sky. And as the stars pierced through the growing darkness, I imagined eternity, my body hurtling through space without end, the Earth tiny, insignificant, forgettable. That night I awakened in bed sweating with fear, the sensation of an empty endlessness coursing through my limbs. The mystery and absolute finality of death had gripped me.

I didn't believe in a hereafter. I was raised without any traditional religious training. My parents had once been Mormons, my mother from a Mormon pioneer family, her mother's father fleeing U.S. marshals, settling finally in Mexico to practice polygamy in the late nineteenth century. But my parents, before I was born, stopped attending church. For years church elders dropped by unannounced to discuss Scripture and bring us back into the fold. They seemed like comic figures to me in their uniformity—black slacks, white shirts, long dark ties, their voices steady and too sincere. Their faith struck me as something quaint left over from distant history. If I was home alone when they knocked, I wouldn't answer. I'd run giggling from the door to the bathroom, where, by standing on the edge of the tub, I could see them out the high window. I grew to think of religion and everything associated with it, including religious painting and music, as slightly foolish.

The week of Grady Gammage Sr.'s funeral, which I did not attend, to regain my equilibrium when seized by death terrors, I created, as if by instinct, my own ritual, a private exorcism. The ritual would prove useful—and necessary—for many years.

Running to my room, lying on my back on the bed whenever the fear struck, feeling as though my body were hurtling through space, through infinity, I'd chant, "Mary had a little lamb whose fleece. . . ." I'd stiffen my arms at my sides, my hands clenched into fists, and shut my eyes tight, chanting the whole verse over and over under my breath until my consciousness was so absorbed in the rhythm and music of the poem, death could find no place in me.

Gradually, I'd feel as if my body were returning, falling from space now toward Earth. Aware finally of where I actually lay, bound to the planet, my arms and eyelids would relax a little and I'd begin an internal journey. My body would feel as if it were shrinking, or as if I had two bodies, one inside the other. The inner body would grow smaller and smaller, falling *into* my real body, into the inner space of my own empty self. I'd begin a new chant to call it back, a counting chant: "onetwothreeonetwothreeonetwothree-onetwothreeonetwo . . ."—until the words were pure sound, a filament of sound running through my veins.

At a point of near unconsciousness, I'd explode into a standing position and walk frantically to and fro in my bedroom, shaking my hands and head to expel the evil feeling of oblivion, anxiety draining from my muscles. If it was night, I could now lie down and sleep. If I'd suffered a daytime terror, I'd look for somebody, anybody I knew, and strike up a conversation in hopes of reentering the normal, unself-conscious rhythm of life.

Permission

"Yes, I'd *love* to. If Mom will let me."

My first ever overnight, and with William, the sight of whose body had strangely stirred me.

Dinner I only partly remember. We sat at a round, massive wooden table and ate something from a mix, a Hamburger Helper casserole or lasagna. His mother was efficient and mechanical. The meal was put on quickly, something stirred and heated and heaped on the plate. My insides squirmed like crazy for fear I'd say or do something dreadful.

I was nine, always trying to make an impression with adults, and my father had told me Dr. Anderson was a physicist. I thought he had to be one of the most brilliant people in the world. Mrs. Anderson didn't speak, a face poised vacantly over her plate. It was all boys talking, William and Dr. Anderson and me and William's younger brother, Brian. Baseball and Sputnik.

But the smells and sights of dinner are buried by the sensations after dinner—our early lights-out and my time under the covers. I'd hoped for something I couldn't put into words. William was lean and had skin so pale it burned in minutes in the summer sun. And his hair was red, a fresh-lit match of hair. He was not only smart in math and science—genes from his father, I reasoned—but the fastest runner in the class and of a graceful thinness, stretched in a way that was delicate, in a way that made me want to embrace him, carefully, protectively, though I knew that was absolute nonsense.

His room was in regular kid disorder, Erector set parts and comic books and baseball gloves and bats. All sorts of stuff piled, crammed, even, into a wall of built-in bookshelves over a built-in painted wooden desk. Not unlike the built-in desk and shelves in my sister's bedroom, though my mother would never have allowed such dishevelment.

And more stuff, dirty clothes, a few plastic dishes, drinking cups of clear colored plastic, between and on the outer sides of twin beds that divided the small square bedroom into thirds.

A sweet smell, sick-sweet, the smell of fig smear I got on my shirttail when I wiped my mouth after eating stolen figs at the back of a neighbor's yard—that's what rose up to my nostrils as I stepped into the room. I didn't mind at first, but when I pulled the covers back, the smell was intense and seemed to come from the sheets, whose surface was darkened, as if a shadow had settled there, from boy perspiration, body oils, body effusions.

This was mid-August, school about to start. I'd joined William earlier that day in the town pool's open showers; I'd noticed the slight rosy shadows around his scrotum while he talked excitedly about his summer vacation in Michigan. And then he'd turned to his father—an enormous pale nakedness I could not look at—for permission, before inviting me to spend the night. So there I was.

"What do you mean, take my clothes off?" I asked. "Of course not. I always sleep in my clothes. Don't you?"

He peeled his shorts down with a shake of his head, then his striped T-shirt over his brow, arms crossed, pulling from the bottom edges upward so that the shirt slipped perfectly inside-out and into a wad that he tossed. My eyes traced those bony shoulders (I wanted to encircle them, like tissue paper around a breakable gift) and those two pink dots, his nipples.

"This will be fine," I said, loosening the heel of a tennis shoe with the opposite toe, then loosening the heel of the other and kicking them free. I drew the covers up to my neck.

"Aren't you gonna be hot?"

"Nah," I said, "we don't even keep our cooler on nights."

He flicked off the light, then knelt by the bed. He prayed, but so I couldn't hear. He threw his covers all the way off and lay on his back, legs spread, arms to the sides. So that every surface, I imagined, could feel the cool of air fall from the overhead vent.

In minutes I could hear steady breathing, and sometimes gulps, sounds I charted, cocooned, sweating through my clothes. I took shallow breaths through my mouth, so as not to smell the sweetness that would make me queasy. I felt an itching over every inch of skin in contact with the sheets—my hands, my arms to the shirtsleeves, the back of my neck.

I became for the first time intimate with the voice of my heart, mechanical but reliable, my other companion, as I watched William sleep through the night. And then watched the growing glow on his skin as sunlight exposed him in delirious increments.

Mr. Todd

The last time I saw Mr. Todd, my high school senior honors English teacher, I was home on Christmas break, 1969, from Oberlin College. I dropped by his house on impulse, pushed the doorbell button, and was greeted by his weathered, complex, expressive face. Bald, short, a squarish trunk atop spindly legs, he possessed a smile that began at the crinkles in the corners of his eyes, mixing, as it lit his features, welcome and sadness and mischief in equal measure. One never knew which emotion would dominate the conversation.

Today he led me into the living room, which was empty, except for the towering portrait of his sixth and current wife. Heir to a Texas oil fortune, she gazed confidently forward, well over our heads, hands in her lap, in a full-length blue satin gown. He motioned me to sit with him in the middle of the room on the pale green carpet.

He had sold the house, he said, and was taking her to Tijuana, for lamb's-blood injections, to cure her of her lethargy.

I didn't question or challenge this. I still considered Mr. Todd, if eccentric, something of a genius. I never saw the woman, though I'd visited their house as a high school senior several times. He would serve me and one or two other honored students cocktails on the patio by the pool, and we'd discuss art and politics, practicing the life of the mind, interweaving Eisenhower and Auden, the Beatles and General MacArthur, into an always unpredictable tapestry of thought. I treasured each moment, struggling at times to keep up with the shifts and turns of conversation.

Having never met his wife, I couldn't help wondering as we sat now in the empty room if she wasn't perhaps a fiction: did he mean to take an actual human to Mexico, or this painting?

Till my last year in high school, I'd found ways to dodge honors English classes. Before my annual advising appointment, I'd outwit my counselor by creating deliberate conflicts in my schedule that would exclude the honors section, a class I was repeatedly urged to join. The fact was, I was terrified of competition in an English class. Since grade school, I'd been intensely competitive in the classroom, even with my closest friends. But writing and literature already meant too much to me in a way different from other subjects to risk comparison with outstanding students. A's were easy in my regular English classes. Not till Mr. Todd, a town legend for his spirited lectures and flamboyant nature, did I take the chance. His class I'd looked forward to for years.

My relationship to him was not without its complications. The first day of class, before the bell rang, he called me to his desk at the head of the room and pointed to the roster of names. "Too many girls," he said, "too many girls. Nothing was ever accomplished by women." His words so stunned me, I walked to my seat feeling dizzy, only half-believing I'd heard what I'd heard. I felt somehow shamed by being the one he had confided in. I didn't know how to tell my parents, or even close friends. During my first weeks in class, I watched for a sign of cruelty or favoritism that might confirm such utter misogyny. Detecting none, I did my best to set the remark aside.

Another incident, which occurred much later, illustrates how confusing his behavior could sometimes be. Close to final exams at the end of the year, the usual distances between student and teacher relaxing for those of us about to graduate, Mr. Todd and I sat down to lunch across from campus at the Burger King. This was novel, a meal in a high school hangout with a teacher. As we started to eat, he launched into a disquisition upon the impossibility of two

Mr. Todd

men ever "succeeding together." I remember those words exactly. He hadn't used the word *homosexual* or *gay* once, but I felt certain, several years before I had a conscious inkling of my own true sexual nature, that he was trying to warn me away from something dreadful. And then he handed me a small paper bag: "Here, you might be able to use these."

That year he had given me books in much the same fashion, books that had made me think in important new ways—Hesse's *Steppenwolf,* Kafka's *The Trial.* Even so, I approached the bag with a peculiar anxiety and didn't open it till I was home alone in my room. Inside were several pairs of sheer, pastel, nylon, men's bikini underwear.

The sight of the see-through underwear made me instantly, inexplicably, nauseous. I brooded several days before going to his house. Instead of confronting him over what a gift of such underwear might signify, I simply handed them back, explaining they weren't my size.

To this day his actions puzzle me. I understand my nausea now—simple fear, my body's automatic response to the truth of what he saw in me, something I hadn't yet consciously acknowledged to myself. But why warn me off from being queer, then give me a present that could only, to my unformed sensibility, represent queerness? Was this a test?

These flashes of eccentricity were painful for me. How reconcile them—and the feelings they called up—with my gratitude for the genius of his teaching, teaching that had introduced me to writing as art?

Two assignments from that year I remember as especially significant. Early in the spring semester he announced that Matthew Arnold's "Dover Beach" was the greatest lyric written in the English language. We were going to study its every word and comma. We were going to memorize and analyze and finally perform this masterpiece, as though it had been written for the stage centuries earlier. We would do it as the ancient Greeks might have, with a chorus, sweeping *strophe* and *counterstrophe*, stage left to right, and right to left, in imitation of the poem/ocean rhythms:

> *the grating roar*
> *Of pebbles which the waves draw back, and fling,*
> *At their return, up the high strand,*
> *Begin, and cease, and then again begin,*
> *With tremulous cadence slow. . . .*

In Greek costume, togas and sandals and wreaths on our heads, we staged the poem beneath a magnificent mulberry off the lunchroom courtyard. One student perched on a branch with a flute to accompany the chorus. Mr. Todd directed with a tambourine. The main solo speaking part was taken by a male student whose voice had entered the adult register, a tall, black-haired, skinny young man with a truly impressive bass. Other English classes that met during our hour were invited as audience.

Aspects of the performance were certainly corny enough—the dress, the grand declamatory style. But measuring our movements to the rhythms of the poem, allowing the music of the lines to enter our muscles, taught us that in poetry, form and content were not so distinguishable as we might have thought. That Arnold created the rhythms of those lines intentionally to give the reader's ear the feel of waves breaking on the shore, that this formal consideration helped produce the power of the poem's meaning, was a revelation.

Shortly after our performance, Mr. Todd stormed out of class. He accused us of laziness, which he called our collective case of senioritis; he would not waste his time teaching young people so utterly lost in indolence. Someone was hired to fill in for him the two weeks that he stayed away.

The year's first assignment had been even more important to

me personally. Mr. Todd asked that we look into our lives for patterns, for the inevitable repetitions. It might be a dream that recurred since childhood, a ritual family celebration, a behavior we saw running through several generations—the subject was essentially open, as long as it demonstrated the theme of repetition.

I knew at once I'd write about my death-terror exorcism, the cycle of chants and body postures and images I created as a child—and still resorted to—in coping with my terror of blank infinity. Not believing in God or heaven, I had a powerful dread of death. For days I struggled to convey the experience in prose, breaking the ritual into paragraphs. I even forced myself to think about death, to grow almost dizzy with fear, as I always did when confronted with oblivion, performing the ritual yet again as a form of research. But nothing I tried on paper succeeded in embodying the obsessive quality of the pattern.

Late on the night before the assignment was due, still frustrated with the essay, which I typed and retyped, hoping the activity might produce some inspiration, I made a momentous decision: I'd disobey the assignment. I knew that Mr. Todd had an explosive disposition, and I was desperate to please him. But the subject demanded a different treatment; the subject demanded I write it as a poem.

And so I began to break apart the paragraphs, working with phrases, cutting explanatory passages, isolating images and important actions. I finally abandoned the left margin, scattering the resulting lines in an e. e. cummings pattern on the pages. All night I pared and revised, working to match the experience to the verbal—and visual—presentation.

I'm sure I trembled as I turned it in. Mr. Todd's response the next week when he returned our papers was shocking. Pacing the room excitedly, arms in the air, he proclaimed me "the child of Mnemosyne," Memory, mother of the muses; I was, he said, "a poet, a true poet." Sitting, finally, at his desk, he commanded me to stand on a small wooden box at the center of the class to perform my work.

Our desks were arranged in a large open rectangle that ran around the outer edges of the room. This way we always faced each other, which made for better discussion. The rectangle was un-broken except at the head of the class, where Mr. Todd's larger desk was positioned.

I paused in my seat, unable to believe the moment was real. Then I took what seemed like a very long walk along the outside of the rectangle to the opening by Mr. Todd. Pivoting toward the center of the floor, I stepped up onto the fruit crate and began to read.

Called by Name

I was four and feverish, cranky but glad to be spending the morning in bed because my mother was reading to me, and then she read:

> *A birdie with a yellow bill*
> *Hopped upon the window-sill,*
> *Cocked his shining eye and said:*
> *"Ain't you 'shamed, you sleepy-head?"*

And I blinked to see where I was—and *who* I was. A scolding bird? A kid in bed the bird was scolding? For an instant, hadn't I been both?

This poem, from Robert Louis Stevenson's *Child's Garden of Verses*, strikes me as direct enough now, more than forty years later. But something huge, something strange, had happened to me that morning. I was for the first time transformed out of my bodily self and into the body of the words. And every time my mother read the poem—and I begged to hear it over and over until I had it memorized—the transformation occurred.

~

After dinner, we'd moved to the living room, dominated by the Steinway baby grand angling toward the middle. Its black lacquer reflected light from the floor lamps at either end of the couch where I sat between my parents. I was nine, keeping up as best I could, thrilled by the crackle of adult voices engaged in lively, serious conversation.

In chairs drawn close to us sat two of my parents' oldest friends. The man was a lawyer, with a long and angular face that made me think of the portrait of Lincoln in my fourth-grade classroom. He'd met his wife, a schoolteacher, at about the time my parents became engaged when they were all in college together in the late 1930s. They were small-town Mormons attending the University of Arizona. With several other couples, they prepared Sunday programs at the campus LDS Institute. My parents, music majors, directed the music; others spoke and gave sermons. Young and idealistic, exposed to a liberal education, they thought eventually they'd be able to change Mormon practices that troubled them. Mormon services, for example, are led by lay ministers, but only white men could enter the priesthood at that time; men of color were excluded. By 1951 when I was born, my parents had moved so far in spirit from the church, I wasn't even baptized.

Was it my imagination, or did their voices grow more subdued as the subject shifted? They'd been discussing the upcoming election between Kennedy and Nixon. But this had led to Nixon's role on the House Committee on Un-American Affairs and the shameful McCarthy hearings in the Senate. Then my father told the story of two colleagues, Jewish musicians on the West Coast. European immigrants, they'd somehow been swept up in the lies and blacklisting that devastated so many artists in the Hollywood film industry. They'd never recovered, professionally or personally.

This was my chance, I thought. I knew some true thing about bias, though I wasn't sure what. I'd just read *The Adventures of Huckleberry Finn*. Since finishing the book I'd walked around feeling both exhilarated and confused. The kind of internal, emotional shift I'd experienced several times as a child when reading, though most often when listening to compelling music—Stravinsky's *Petrouchka,* for example, or "Dido's Lament" from the Purcell opera *Dido and Aeneas.* But music was music and nothing beyond itself, pure sound. No use trying to puzzle out how it moved me, what it might mean.

My response to the novel I could not so easily put aside. At the point Huck makes his dramatic vow—"All right, then, I'll *go* to hell"—I had actually burst out sobbing, my body convulsing as if a long-concealed pain had been released. Why Huck's decision to accept damnation, which he sincerely believes will mean "everlasting fire," rather than turn in his friend Jim, a runaway slave; why this recognition, that he must trust his feelings for Jim, his experience of Jim's humanity, rather than do what he's been taught is right by the people he thinks of as good, like the churchgoing Widow Douglas; why this should leave me so shaken, though so gladdened, I had no answer for.

I don't remember what I said that evening about the novel. I do remember that my parents' friends seemed impressed I'd read it. All agreed this was not just a child's book, but could be appreciated at any age and on many levels.

⁓

Reading *Huck Finn* in high school and then in college, I came to appreciate Huck's courage in embracing the truth about what he must do; I was stirred by the beauty, the complication, of that arrival, which I recognized as both burden and deliverance. But each time I read it, I had the same response at the point of Huck's vow, the same feeling of a deep and secret pain released. Eventually I formed an image of the experience: it was as if a fish, beached and gasping

beside a river, had been slipped back into the water, restored to life
by return to its natural element.

In 1974, a new MFA graduate student in the University of Arizona
English Department, I was given a choice of novels to teach in my
composition course. "Teach best what you love most," I'd heard my
faculty supervisor say. *The Adventures of Huckleberry Finn* was on
the list of Norton Critical Editions. I still have my complimentary
teacher's desk copy. The pages have yellowed along the borders to a
warm, Rhode Island hen's-egg brown, lightening about an inch and
a half from the edge to a creamy paleness. The text, framed by the
darker color, stands out, nearly glows, like words on a computer
screen.

The book falls open to page 168, where Huck makes his vow.
Throughout are ink stars and check marks in the margins, underlin-
ing and bracketed passages, whole sentences boxed in (I guess I
hadn't caught on to highlighters twenty-five years ago), scribbled
notations ("always physical comfort" on page 9, "as if in heaven:
Angel of Death" on page 34), and so on.

My supervisor hadn't warned me about what hurts most:
students not caring for what you love. The humor, the dialects,
the boundless ironies—my pep talks and Socratic lectures, nudging
students to embrace the novel, failed to spark much enthusiasm.
We finally took to reading passages aloud.

This had worked during the poetry unit. Earlier in the semester, collective groans greeted my distribution of syllabus pages
outlining our study of poetry. But it never occurred to me *not* to
read poems aloud. From the first day, when I read Sylvia Plath's
"Daddy"—

You do not do, you do not do
Any more, black shoe

In which I have lived like a foot

For thirty years, poor and white,

Barely daring to breathe or Achoo . . .

—then, for contrast, Theodore Roethke's "Elegy for Jane"—

I remember the neckcurls, limp and damp as tendrils;

And her quick look, a side-long pickerel smile;

And how, once startled into talk, the light syllables leapt for her,

And she balanced in the delight of her thought,

A wren, happy, tail into the wind . . . ·

they were engaged.

    We began with Huck's very first sentences:

> *You don't know about me, without you have read a book by the name of "The Adventures of Tom Sawyer," but that ain't no matter. That book was made by Mr. Mark Twain, and he told the truth, mainly. There was some things he stretched, but mainly he told the truth. That is nothing. I never seen anybody but lied, one time or another, without it was Aunt Polly, or the Widow Douglas, or maybe Mary.*

Who could help but be charmed by this disarmingly fresh and sly boy? Hearing—experiencing the actual sound of his voice—made all the difference. (And who, as a writer, could help but be struck by how contemporary the opening is: a fictional character naming his author and the earlier novel in which he, the character, first came to life?) For the remainder of the unit, we selected key passages for daily reading aloud. I took turns with student volunteers; several worked up small plays where dialogue takes over, though these ended up somewhat contrived. Regardless, that they were listening to a complex human narrator, that this was the *experience* of a story and not merely a book to be mined for hidden meaning, changed their relationship to the novel.

There was no question but that I'd claim pages 166 through 168 for myself. I worked on them in my small studio apartment, standing and addressing the wall behind the door screwed to table legs that served as my desk. I was concerned as to how I'd handle the climactic moment. I'd given several poetry readings and discovered that my role as performer distanced me from the sometimes emotional nature of the material. Bad enough that comics should laugh at their own jokes; heaven help us if poets start weeping when reading their own poems.

I thought I was ready. But I broke the sentence in two. No actual sobs, but that unmistakable wobble in the voice and welling at the eyes. I tried to cover. Still shaken, I asked an obvious question to gain distance, something like "Have you ever known you'd have to do something that everybody else, even the people you care for most, think is wrong?" My students weren't buying it. No response. Nor, however, were they giggling. They waited in silence. Good for them. I told them what I could, that for some reason this passage had always torn me up. That, though I was a poet, this novel had been more important to me than any other piece of writing. And this was the spot in the novel that always got me.

There was something else in my mind at that moment, as close to an epiphany as I've ever experienced. Self-knowledge for me is generally a slow process, a matter of accretion, layer upon layer of experience leading me inexorably to what may seem obvious to so many others. This flash of insight I did not share with my students. I had automatically, silently, in my mind, answered my own clumsy question: "Have you ever known you'd have to do something. . . ."

At that precise moment in my life, my first year of graduate school, I'd finally recognized what many of my friends had known for some time: I am a gay man. I have not the slightest doubt that, despite the years of girlfriends and heterosexual ritual I engaged in, I have always been gay. The unwinding of experience leading to that understanding is another story. What I finally realized about *Huck Finn,* however, about the power of great art altogether, is its ability to prepare the way for us to know ourselves, to call us by name before we can know we've been called. I have no doubt that my boy self recognized in some unchartable, unconscious manner that, like Huck, what I was was supposed to be wrong, if not down-right evil. In the minds of many, it still is.

THREE

Taboo

"Nothing human disgusts me unless it's unkind."

Mercy, how that line thrilled me. *This* is what the writer must aspire to, I thought, twisting it slightly in my mind: nothing human *is beyond* me. . . .

The line was delivered, circa 1964, by Hannah (played by Deborah Kerr), who tended her dying poet-father in a village on the Gulf of Mexico. Hannah's love life, she confided, had consisted of an adolescent knee touch in a nearly empty movie house and a man she shared a shaky sampan with, an Aussie tourist she met on the Straits of Malacca. He asked that she remove her panties so that he might hold them while masturbating. The scene is reenacted in flashback in the film *The Night of the Iguana*—from the play by Tennessee Williams, who boasted in his *Memoirs* of sweeping a ragged boy from a cafe in Rome, scrubbing him up, and buggering all winter long. "Nothing human disgusts me."

Hannah confirmed what I knew instinctively: the writer must embrace the heart's darkest places. One must be protean, all forms of humanity, capable of imagining oneself as anything, not just the easy stuff—movie star, Nobel in science, savior of one's people. Artists had to lick the veritable butt-crack of life, Verlaine- and Rimbaud-style. "I could kill," I practiced like a mantra, "eat human flesh, fuck a goat, if I had to."

Eighteen, a permanent hard-on in my jeans, how might I turn what I loved doing most into utter vileness, I wondered, to expand my soul? Then a flash, confirming my genius: I'd have sex with my mother. Not in the flesh, mind you. If I could beat off with dear old Mom in my mind's story, I'd move on to my sister, my brother (piece of cake), perhaps my father. Then the killing could begin.

In a fever from flu, home from college on Christmas break, I squinted as my mother switched the hall light on, tiptoed in, then leaned to touch my forehead. The pull of gravity: her gown sagged—bloop—at the top, and two dark nipples bobbed. *Like giant brown eraser heads,* I thought in horror before I could clamp my eyes shut. A sight I'll never have the power of imagination to forget.

⁓

Broke after graduate school, I lived with friends and their four-year-old boy in a rented house. My room at the very back had been their den, which had been till recently a covered patio. The landlords closed it in, retaining the sliding glass door that led from patio to dining room.

This was 1977, a tad past *Playboy*'s prime. But the Hefner aesthetic seemed to inform the landlords' sense of interior design. Blood-red shag carpet stretched wall to wall. The walls they'd paneled in dungeon-dark fake mahogany. A bar stood at one end, with a set of three high wrought-iron stools; behind the bar, to match the paneling, was a fake mahogany cabinet with glass doors and shelves. Over my bed hung the crowning touch: a gilded, neo-Victorian, New Orleans whorehouse ceiling fan.

I spent the first two months in a funk, out of work, no money to find a boyfriend at the bars, hardly enough sex drive left to even bother beating off. I lay day after day in bed reading nothing but Chandler and Hammett mysteries. Hard dames. Hard drinking. Double crosses. My friends' boy would haul the sliding door back unannounced. He'd bounce up on the bed, poke me in the belly, and ask to wrestle. We'd tumble in the sheets, then onto the carpet. I

Taboo

was so much bigger, I had to encircle him with my body, making sure I didn't snap his tender limbs.

I'd tickle at the end, till he cried uncle. And then we'd bound off to the kitchen for a snack. The boy seemed pleased to have a grown-up playmate in the house. I noticed, though, that sometimes in wrestling I'd get half-erect, my brief happiness turning instantly to shame. No job, living off the kindness of friends, was bad enough; getting hard-ons with their child—I was disgusted with my-self. I decided we'd best play word games or draw on construction paper up at the bar, which I'd made my writing desk.

In a few months, finding employment as a motel desk clerk, I earned enough to move out. Then, home one afternoon from work, I discovered my little friend had left a Halloween present with a parent-assisted scrawl—"Love, K"—at the doorstep of my new apart-ment. The present was some kind of art project he'd made in his pre-school. He'd painted a shoebox all black, then cut a two-by-five-inch slot in the top.

I took the box to my kitchen table but couldn't pry the lid off. Glued tight. Shining a flashlight into the slot, I saw a tiny plastic sol-dier, stuck on his back to the floor of the box. It looked like he lay in a swirl of glue, which was clotted in places where the boy had sprinkled sand. But as I angled the flashlight to get a better view, here and there I could see the brilliant sparkle of blue and silver glit-ter all around the soldier, as if he lay in a bed of stars.

To Dusk

"And then it *dawned* on me. . . ."

I think of the accretions of light that my friends and I could not see but could not deny as we awaited sunrise following summer all-night parties, our parents away on family business or one of their "no kids" holidays. Between our town and Phoenix to the north there was a small desert park. A bubbling of red rock hills, interwoven at their bases by dirt roads that ran alongside riparian habitats—a pattern of ponds linked by streams, threading desert willows, cottonwoods, and reeds over several square miles.

Our car lights washed over the greens as we took the many irregular turns, a crunching of tires filling our ears, the radio off. After a five-minute navigation to the park's heart, we'd stop at the base of a familiar sandstone rise. The click-swing-thunk of car doors punctuated the gravelly sentence we'd made through the landscape. First, silence. Then, as our ears adjusted to the stillness, crickets, the huffing of breezes through underbrush, off to one side a bullfrog, some yip-yips followed by the high narrow braiding of coyote songs.

Looking up, you could just make out "Hole-in-the-Rock," a thousand-square-foot oval room carved into the hilltop like a giant eye socket. The rise from this side, thirty yards, was too steep to safely climb. We scrambled instead at an angle, up and to the right, circling to the hill's back. Hauling ourselves over several final boulders, we emptied through a crack into the room. Gazing out the front, out the enormous open oval, it seemed we viewed all of eternity: dark and infinite, the inky night sky. I'd sit at the opening's very edge, trying to observe the unobservable, the increments of approaching daylight.

⌒

A dawning. The slow way, at times, we arrive at an important understanding. The child, over several years, discerns a household transformation: parents not embracing; a mother's more frequent phone calls to her favorite sister; a father's longer days at work. A change the child cannot measure the way he does his summer catch, notching with a penknife a willow branch each time he pulls a bass from the lake; a change he feels deepening by incalculable degrees, the blood draining so slowly from the face, the body, the premise of *family*, he cannot hope to arrest the loss.

But why no figure of speech for the opposite, the gentling fall of light, the way darkness soaks through the landscape at day's end? How else describe so much that happens to so many of us as we age, the dispersal of our worldly ambitions, the bemusement as the hair thins, the waist expands, as we forget where we put this or that? Rather than feel impatient with the impatience of friends in their twenties who declare, "I'll die if I don't get to . . . I'd kill for the chance to . . . ," we're charmed, we wish them well; in them we see, without the stain of jealousy, a hope beyond ourselves. We raise a toast. The gin is dry, invigorating. How come we never took the time before to savor the pleasant way it lends this lightness to our limbs? The silence that comes at endings—the symphony's last chord, the play's final word—provides release. How could we have wasted so much, we wonder, on trivial fears—that we might never find love, or fame, or worse. . . .

The breeze is cool, the softness permeates all things, at the time of day when struggles cease. A life, like the idea of a life, may be said to dusk.

To Dusk

67

Care

My father lives in a nursing home. Over eighty, with pure white feathery hair, he sits curled up like a snail, except he has no shell to shape or protect him. Instead, from the inside, his spine, ever tightening, locks him in a twisted forward dive over his own lap. His recliner must be tilted far back so that he can look out at the world.

In so many ways his life has narrowed. For over a year he's been too weak to hold the large-print books that line his shelves. For a time he could grasp a magazine upright in his hands. He used to work his way through *Time* and the *New Yorker,* checking off articles he thought others would enjoy. But now even magazines seem too cumbersome. And TV doesn't interest him. His greatest remaining pleasure is music. Not surprising, considering he taught piano and harpsichord for nearly forty years. Though he needs powerful hearing aids for conversation, he takes them out to listen to cassettes through headphones.

As for movement, with the buttons attached to a cord resting on his lap, he can extend or drop the leg props of his electric recliner; raise or lower the seat; raise or lower the seat-back. Gripping a walker, bent double at the waist, his head looped almost to his knees, he can take several shaky steps—from recliner to wheelchair, wheelchair to bed.

Beyond visits by me and other family members at irregular intervals, including his birthday and Christmas, my father spends his days listening to tapes, dozing, rousing for meals, and, for two hours, three times a week, conversing with the "friend" we've hired.

Two years ago he lived in a group home. Back then, bent merely at a right angle, he moved room to room with confidence using his walker. When I'd visit, we'd sit in his bedroom and talk about what we were reading; we'd talk about the past—he had several photo albums we'd flip through; he'd ask about my life on the outside: Was my partner, Gary, working on any new paintings? What was growing in our garden? Did I bring poems to show him? Then he'd tell me some new story concerning Mira, the large, whiskered woman in her fifties who managed the home. How she'd been kept up two nights nursing a resident through illness, how she'd found the time to make a rice pudding just for him.

During most of his eighteen months there, all five of the other residents were women, and all but one intensely senile. My father called them "dames," a word that burst from his lips with a snarl. Arranged in a semicircle in the common room, they sat in recliners every day watching *Oprah,* their favorite, and the other talk shows before and after. My father, his recliner at the semicircle's center, would read, hearing aids turned all the way down. He said he couldn't bear these women, but as far as I know, he never chose anywhere to read but among them.

Mira, who tended them all, cooking meals, helping them to chairs, the bathroom, the dining table, helping each to bathe on a rotation posted in the hallway to the bedrooms—Mira was, in my father's words, "a marvelous gal, and a saint." "I don't see how she puts up with those dames," he'd snap. Then, his eyes moist, voice softening, "She deserves better."

One day my father offered her the gift of a black opal pendant and matching ring. No matter they belonged to his second wife, to whom he'd given them twenty-five years earlier. A woman

Care

69

who remained his most devoted friend following their divorce, visiting the group home several times each week.

Yesterday I met my father's new favorite at the nursing home, a woman of remarkable heft, fine brown hair pinned loosely atop a head too small for such a massive body. Though my mother and my father's second ex are slender, as wiry and upright in bearing as he is compressed, staff at a nursing home must be substantial enough to lift, many times each day, the often enfeebled men and women who live there—from beds, wheelchairs, toilet seats, baths. The staff all wear black lifter's belts, like exterior corsets, over their matching pale blue nylon shirts and trousers.

Strolling the halls, I hear the cries and groans, the calls for help, the rhythmic humming, counting, nonsense-syllable repetitions. All commonplace, expected, in such places. I also hear grunts, the sounds of straining, as staff lift the bodies of their living charges. It took me several visits to locate the source of these sounds.

Blanche and my father call each other "Sweetie," "Honey," "Dear." He asks for a kiss; she pecks him dryly on the forehead or cheek. Her smile reveals a wild disorder—just a scattering of teeth, though she can't be over forty, each tooth of an independent bent, literally. Blanche leans so that my father can return the favor, his face so bright, his cheeks raised so high, his eyes are slits.

Blanche gives my father commands without sounding mechanical or uninterested: "Stand on the count of three," lifting from under an arm; "Now turn," steadying him with a grip on the waistband of his pants. When he settles, finally, into the recliner with a grimace—virtually no move he makes goes unrewarded by a jolt of pain—she expertly tucks the pillows, each rolled or folded or bunched in a particular fashion, and positions the blankets and Kleenex in the ways he requires, a routine developed over the past

Care

70

several years. One piece out of place and he'll fidget until somebody rights the error. "Only Blanche," he assures me, "gets everything right." The job complete, he is encased in softness.

Yesterday I also learned that their relationship has been formalized by the state. The tilt of his head, the slightly lofty, mocking tone of his voice, warned me the tale would reveal some irony. To avoid even the slightest appearance of improper conduct, Blanche and my father were required to sign sworn statements declaring their affection is mutual, uncoerced, nonsexual. He took obvious delight in recreating the scene: arrayed behind the recliner, the three blue-clad, corseted nursing home attendants who served as witnesses; ensconced in pillows and blankets at the center, my father, Blanche standing at his side; the two, gazing into one another's eyes, reciting, like bride and groom, their solemn vows, before signing the papers.

The Touch

"Some people just have it," my young friend, a former poetry student, tells me. We've poked our heads into a blanket-draped closet that he calls his grow room. He's rigged it up with special lights on timers and a fan. "People used to say 'green thumb.' Now it's vibrations, So-and-so has the right vibrational level, no kidding," he says, his voice rising to the strangeness of what he's about to reveal.

It seems he read about an experiment in which a scientist walked through a room filled with plants, hacking off leaves and branches. The plants were hooked up to sensors, which all went nuts, measurements off the wall, like the plants were screaming. When he left the room, everything settled down. When he walked back in, the plants started up again, as if they remembered the guy.

"Of course, they didn't remember him," my friend explains, "but they knew his vibrations from the last time. See what I mean? He could even go into rooms where the plants had never seen him before and they'd get hysterical. So I figure I just don't have the right vibrational level," he concludes, pointing sadly to his marijuana sprouting pots, which have no sprouts.

Which reminds me of the experiment I read about. In this one plants in I don't know how many rooms were set up with all the same conditions—soil and water and light and nutrients and temperature, everything identical. But into each room was piped a different kind of music. One got ZZ Top, another Mozart, another Zappa, another Ellington, another Staukhausen. It turned out nothing compared to Mozart. Plants in that room grew greener, taller, had better self-concepts, better sex. I was disappointed they didn't try Schubert, though some of his music is so ethereal, like the poems of Rilke, who wasn't much of a gardener, I suppose the tomatoes would tend toward wanness.

My mother thrives on Bach, especially when she's doing yoga. She's also a vegetarian. It's all been incredibly good for her, this combination of Baroque music, yoga, and the right food. Now she's eighty-one, as lean and upright as a Corinthian column, with pale blue eyes that never stop laughing. She can stand on her head for days, and has the circulation of a sixteen-year-old. Her doctor writes her up in medical journals; her guru has her demonstrate headstands in workshops from Bali to Jamaica.

One thing she can't give up entirely, though, is bacon. When she first turned vegetarian twenty-five years ago, it was the last flesh she ate. Somehow breakfast just wasn't breakfast without that sizzling, salty, crunchy meat. Then one morning she said she started frying up a batch and just like that, *bam!*—it smelled like shit. Not as a figure of speech, mind you, but actual shit. If she could eat that, she figured she might as well start shopping for groceries in public toilets.

That all changed eight years later when she had a little problem with her masseur, who was also one of her yoga students. His own body was so tied in knots she had to rig up every prop in the house, all kinds of pillows, rolled blankets, specially shaped objects she orders from The *Yoga Journal,* just to get him into basic poses, passive ones where you position yourself a certain way and let gravity take your body's weight, pulling you in useful directions.

But he seemed to have the touch. His hands could play her body's muscles, organs, and skin like a great pianist revealing the inner truths of a Beethoven sonata.

My father was a pianist. My mother divorced him after twenty years. Sometimes great music-making's not enough. My father, good man that he was, had a very old-fashioned sense of how a wife should conduct herself. But you can't put a straitjacket on a woman with the soul of a samurai and expect her to perform the tea ceremony without eventually spilling a little.

In the end the masseur said something that reminded my mother of my father, something insulting to her samurai soul. More *how* he said the thing than what he said. Some echo of a premise in his tone: "Oh, Louise, the trouble with you is. . . ." It happened while she was under his hands, naked and lotioned and trusting and re-laxed; trying to become more so, as he worked her over. It was all she could do to keep from shaking right off the sheets and onto the floor.

She made it through the massage somehow; the anger had not yet risen into words. That can take twenty years. This time twenty-four hours did the trick. She fired up her '79 Mustang at the crack of dawn, picked up a pound of bacon at a nearby all-night market, cooked herself a fragrant, tasty helping, then another. Felt better. Kept turning the matter over. Had a Coke with lunch. Felt even better. Then called the masseur for the pleasure of treating him to a verbal roasting. After which she placed the remaining uncooked bacon in the freezer.

Now when I'm contemplating a visit, I call the night before to test the waters, managing always to inquire, "So whatcha been hav-ing for breakfast lately?"

Manners

I'd stepped onto that bus in Phoenix feeling gigantically ready for the world to fill me. Twenty, tall and lean, college-savvy, in my beloved worn jeans and faded green corduroy shirt. I strode to the last open pair of seats, each thump of my boot heels like a shot of adrenaline all through me. I was ready for this slow trip cross-country to friends and summer work in New York City. I was going by bus to see the country, to feel its rhythms, to take possession of it. I slid over to the window.

The bus trembled with each step of the man who got on last. A urine and garbage stench rolled out before him. A thundering four-hundred-pound human Dumpster. Clothes, layers and layers, all grime-grays and holes and oily shreds. Green rheum spilled from an eye; from his mouth, a hoarse chuffing with each sideways thrust down the aisle. Heads turned, bodies leaned toward windows, fingers quickly scattered things over empty spaces. In front of me, a white-haired old man sprawled suddenly across two seats, pretending to sleep.

I was pinned to the window. Quick clipped breaths. I stifled a gag, then breathed through my mouth, the bus groaning backwards from the terminal. Sucking the bus exhaust couldn't be worse, I thought. I thought, *I gotta move inside myself*. Like I do on long hikes. Climbing from the Colorado River, mile after mile, to the Grand Canyon rim—the heft of the pack, the soak of sweat, legs rhythmically pumping, the beat of the heart, the body crawls into the mind: *don't look up, you'll get there, you'll get to the top . . .*

"Are you okay?"

I'd never heard a sweeter voice. High and trembly; sincere. As if the wretched flesh enveloped a concerned little girl.

It brought me back to myself; it'd been hours since we'd left Phoenix. My eyes had been open to the passing landscape, but what swept before me had failed to register. I'd imagined instead an endless razor-wire extending from my gaze, severing, like a sci-fi movie laser, everything to the horizon. Phone poles and roadside Texaco billboards and whole stands of palo verdes and abandoned pump stations and random tin-roofed houses; the world toppling, neatly sliced, as we passed. I'd been on a sweaty endless summer Sunday ride to visit relatives, trapped in the back seat, sealed off from the conversations of adults up front.

"Yeah, but I need to pee," I lied, and tried to stand up. Hunched under the overhead rack, I was shocked at my height.

"Let me let you by," offered the voice of the girl. Then the whole bulk huffed upward, filling the aisle, making a space for me to slip out.

Ground

A nature photographer once repositioned a branch he couldn't quite reach with his camera lens. On it a nest, a bird, a bit of wing-beating beauty he wished to capture. If he could just lower the branch six inches, the angle would be perfect, the mother bird, her tireless feeding of the little ones, beaks gaping upward. He'd re-attach the branch once he'd gotten his photos.

But the mother, away on worm-gathering errands, could not find home when she returned. Over and over she circled the spot where she'd left her babies. Wild with the strangeness of their absence, she could not see *home* because it couldn't be *home* six inches down and to the left.

Gaze into a reversing mirror so that the face's right half becomes its left and vice versa, so that the nose's lifelong bias to the one side is suddenly its opposite. "Could these features be mine?" you'll wonder.

I try to snap the chain of synapses, the triggering paths of habits in my brain. Start small, I figure. No more locking the bike to the same metal post, the one painted green, row six, third from the sidewalk, outside the building where I teach Thursday mornings. Try the building's other side, try one of the rows not in afternoon shade. This is winter; the warmth of the black leather seat will feel good on the ride home.

But after class I draw an absolute blank. In a panic I gather my students to help me as they tumble from the building. "I'm not even sure of its color," I confess. I've owned it too long to see it.

A habit that slips out of consciousness becomes a premise, a form of forgetting. "What's wrong?" a friend asks, pulling her shopping basket alongside mine at the supermarket. She touches the furrows on my brow, which immediately flatten.

Inside I'm all cool river, an idle fantasy as I pluck items from shelves: "Dear Mr. Rickel," writes the *New Yorker* poetry editor, "I'm pleased to inform you . . ."—my forbidding brow an unconscious posture . . . against what, the Muzak, a stranger's idle question?

For many, a job is a premise, a home; or a family, a friend, a beloved dog. And then a business fails, a house burns down; a mother dies, a confidant, a woolly pal. An inner hollow opens. "Be in advance of all parting," Rilke recommends.

What would we be without them, these premises? They form an interior ground; on it the scaffold of selfhood stands. But once the ground gives, what holds us up? Best enter the absence, look around, before that time comes, before the hollow widens and you slip into free-fall.

Unknown sounds sent my father into free-fall. He worked, half-sleepless, night after night in each new house—five by the time I was nine—tracking them down. A classical musician, a master of harpsichord, with a flashlight he'd sweep the corners of hallways and closets, tapping the walls, seeking the source of creaking joists. He'd open faucets in various combinations, the thunk and clank of waterworks to his ear a nightmarish timpani, repose's enemy. Tracing the vector of air from a cooler vent, he'd shake the shower curtain to know the sound of its shimmy. We'd hear him outside our bedroom windows testing tree limbs, swooshing the bushes.

When the research was complete, when he'd named and mapped the precise location and temper of every household utterance, when he'd internalized each, made each a premise, made each into silence, he'd proclaim with satisfaction the morning after, "My sleep was sound."

Chaos

They were once the flesh and bone of him. Our beloved friend. Of course, the flesh and bone were not him, even when alive. I rubbed the ashes, gritty white and gray granules, firmly between my fingers; their edges could draw blood.

I leaned to say goodbye. Said goodbye. Kissed the lips I'd kissed so many times, especially the last six days when friends and family sat round the clock talking and holding his hands, massaging his limbs. His eyes grew larger as he diminished, the skin retracting, his graying hair and beard taking on prominence. I thought his face—the features modeled, simplified—a perfect form, like the face of Peter in the frescoes by Giotto; I felt an inner distancing at such a thought and told no one.

But once he was dead—Gary and I got the call just before eleven in the morning and reached his bed in twenty minutes— there was no presence in that flesh, just some powerful sense he was nearby. And so I spoke my final words to the flesh—held his hand, kissed his lips, his forehead—but felt my sentences taken up elsewhere, around the body, in the air.

So all the fuss of how to dispose of the ashes, all the ceremony we created: brilliant flowered wrapping paper cut into squares and folded into palm-size envelopes; the ashes in an aluminum bowl laid on the ground, on a bright red kitchen cloth, just off the Aspen Trail, up in the grove he loved; August, the leaves dull gold now that clouds closed in over our heads, above the towering treetops; the mountaintop a mile in the air at the northeast edge of Tucson, up a winding twenty-five-mile road in five cars with all our dogs; his partner and a dozen of his closest friends holding hands in a circle, taking turns telling stories; a passing of the bowl and silver serving spoon; each scooping some of the coarse, tiny human shards; the hollow scudding sound as the ashes slid into the flowered envelopes; the human circle breaking finally, like slow atoms of a single molecule spreading randomly into the woods; finding places to scatter the ashes; and then, one by one, returning to the circle, the molecule's atoms rejoining, in a new configuration.

One friend tucked her envelope of ashes into her purse; a portion was set aside for his partner to bury in their garden; a portion held out for family in New York where he was born. A minor fragmentation, a temporary holding of small concentrations, to be dispersed elsewhere—which left me oddly unsettled.

I know no concentration endures, human or otherwise. Things do fall apart, scatter, like discarded domestic objects: a one-quart stainless-steel pot from a wedding set, in which a wife cooked a portion of her first household meals, becomes one of many gifts when her son sets up his first apartment in college; becomes a gift again, years later, when the son, no longer single, buys, with his partner, their first matched cookwear, the odds and ends from their families and thrift-store student pasts, sent off to a charity's second-hand outlet—except the one, the pot that was his mother's, which he held back, saved for the day he could give it to someone else; a new young friend, a poet, who lives on air and string.

I see the pot when I visit with him in the kitchen of his new apartment; we're discussing a villanelle by Elizabeth Bishop, which opens, "The art of losing's not hard to master." He lifts the pot from the flame—he's made a vegetable sauce that needs to cool for dinner later—and much to my horror, plonks it directly into the freezer.

Last week on our back porch at dusk, this young friend blurted, a little in his cups from whiskey-and-7's and apropos of what I don't recall, "I read about chaos theory. It only takes ten years for the piss you flushed yesterday to come full circle. The molecules disperse, they spread out all over the world. Then one morning you turn the faucet, and some of those molecules fall right out in your drinking water!"

No, no, how's that chaos? I wanted to protest, also a little in my cups, yet startled by my sudden emotion. How's that chaos when they return to us as something else?

FOUR

Brown Boys

1

I find it impossible to remember the first dark-skinned boy, the one that led to another that led to another, from the mid-1970s to the early eighties. As well to begin with Pablo in spring of 1975.

Three angels, I thought instantly upon entering Jekyll and Hyde's that night, spotting the three lovely dark boys grouped opposite the door. I'd arrived early this evening, a quarter to nine. I wanted a good seat for the drag show at ten o'clock. I positioned myself on a barstool with care, one foot on the floor, the other on the chrome footrest.

I was startled to see one of the boys at my side. When he spoke, he drew each word out slightly, with just a trace of accent: "You want to join us?" His gaze was riveting, his irises black and twice framed—by the whites of his eyes and the identical black arcs of his lashes, above and below.

"Sure," I said to the air, hurrying to catch the quick-footed messenger.

"I'm Miguel," he said as I drew up beside him, "and *thees*"— his accent more noticeable, his voice rising for emphasis—"my friends, Pablo"—gesturing with a sweep of his arm like a waiter indicating an available chair—"and Geraldo." The tallest, his back to us, half-twisted to nod.

I extended my hand to Pablo, as much to touch him as to observe custom. His skin was astonishingly smooth, his expression so sweet, so open, my mouth dried instantly, cottony with desire.

And then a quick, inexplicable drama played out. Geraldo whirled from his stool, stomping out of the bar. Miguel rattled something sharply in Spanish to Pablo, and back and forth the two boys talked in bursts, with laughter and *Ooh la*'s and one low whistle from Miguel following the only word I could catch: "Geraldo."

I tried to read their expressions. I grinned stupidly from face to face as the two youths carried on in a world apart.

I would become only too familiar with this dilemma in the next few years, experiencing it to one degree or another almost every time I met someone sexually desirable in a bar. Nearly always he was Hispanic, often as not a Mexican national; and young, at the juncture of genders, for whom "girlish" and "boyish" were equally applicable—and with whom conversation was equal parts earnest nods and smiles and disjointed English phrases. In the smoke and vague light of gay bars, my eyes zeroed in on them unfailingly. I didn't know why and didn't much care. One's erotic attractions were obviously instinctive. What amazed me was how often the youths I desired returned my gaze.

New to gay bars at twenty-three, raised by my parents, both classical musicians, to an Old World level of decorum, I turned absurdly formal in this uninhibited realm. I trembled each time I approached Jekyll's door. I usually couldn't speak till I'd downed three or four beers.

I was new not only to the bars but to knowledge of my own homosexuality. From junior high through college, I'd had one steady girlfriend after another. With some I'd discussed marriage. My attraction to men I'd suppressed, sealed since adolescence in masturbation fantasies I could dip into at will—fantasies that vanished from consciousness as soon as I'd come. Only in the last months of college did my sexual feelings for men begin to surface, and then only tentatively, in my waking daily life.

Everything broke open one drunken night at a college graduation party. A young man I'd known casually—we had been waiters in the same dining hall—flirted openly with me. Feeling adventurous and flattered, I returned his attention. We danced off and on in a dense swirl of bodies. That in the celebration we pressed against one another, a man and a man, seemed to matter to nobody. When the party ended, he invited me to his dorm room.

The experience was immediately transforming. Though awkward, too teethy, with too little patience, and literally shaking with fear, I felt a profound and undeniable rightness in the sexual kinship of our bodies. So *this* explained the ghostly guilt that lurked inside me, the sense that I held some part of myself in reserve, involuntarily, whenever a relationship with a woman grew serious.

After several terrible moments of attending Miguel and Pablo's conversation, I stepped toward the bar, motioning for a bartender in hopes of breaking the spell of my panic.

Miguel tugged at my arm. "Let's find seats." He nodded toward the small sunken amphitheater where the drag shows were held. "Don't mind Geraldo," he added. "She's in *love*." I ordered beers for myself and my new acquaintances.

The top two tiers of seats were already jammed. We managed to squeeze in on the bottom, thigh to thigh, Pablo in the middle. Miguel and I did the talking at first, leaning across Pablo, who pushed back into the knees of those in the row above to make room. When I told Miguel I taught writing as a graduate student at the University of Arizona, he joked that I could do their homework for classes at the junior college. He and his two friends had come from the small town of Madera in northern Mexico to study English—and to get away from their families. Miguel, whose English was best, had arrived several weeks early to find an apartment and figure things out about summer school.

"My sisters need a little watching," Miguel said, patting Pablo on the shoulder.

Having literally no gay friends, having rarely conversed with any gay man for more than a few minutes in a bar, a few minutes in bed, and the car ride between, I found this use of *sisters,* even the casual substitution of *she* for *he,* oddly charming.

"I *love* those girls," Miguel said, turning toward the stage. The mistress of ceremonies, Lady Lazarus, and another figure had just slipped from the restrooms to a changing-screen at the back of the stage.

"You've been here before?"

"Nearly every night for two weeks. *This* girl." Miguel pulled back to look at Pablo. "I was good till *she* came to town. Now it's go! go! go!"

Pablo said something to Miguel in Spanish, poking him in the ribs, then slid his arm around my waist. I pressed my leg a little more into his.

"He wants to know what lies I'm telling," Miguel said.

"Yes. I not know to speak . . . I. . . ."

"We . . . all . . . *eh*student," Miguel mocked.

"You're doing great," I said, resting a hand on Pablo's knee.

The show was about to begin. The lights dropped, and a crackly recorded trumpet fanfare announced Lady Lazarus. In a floor-length green satin gown, a diamond rhinestone tiara at an angle atop her wig of red ringlets, she swept into a shaft of light. A bartender on a high ladder directed by hand the stage's only spot.

"Who says we're not proud to be queens?" Lady Lazarus rasped, straightening her tiara to a roar of applause and hoots from the audience. "Now tame down, all you hunks, or I'll just have to call *the Man* to put you in your place."

A mixture of boos and chants of "The Man! The Man!"

Onto stage strutted someone not much over five feet tall in full police regalia—Dandy Dan, a well-known local leather dyke.

"Bring 'em *all* on!" cooed Lady Lazarus, gliding from the

stage as three of the bar's male bartenders lined up behind Dandy Dan, each in a different male drag—biker, lumberjack, and phone repairman.

Two floodlights at the corners of the stage flicked on, from the speakers the Village People began to sing, and the four performers marched resolutely in place, lip-synching the lyrics to "Macho Man."

Pablo, when the lights dropped, proved not the least shy. He began rubbing the small of my back. I slid a hand along his inner thigh. Grinning blindly in the direction of the stage, I felt him shift his weight. Then he leaned to kiss my neck, moving quickly to my lips.

How many times in recent months had I seen two men necking like this in a gay bar and thought it crude.

"Bitsy! Bitsy! Bitsy!" the audience chanted.

Our seats shook to the rhythm. A tiny Hispanic queen in a red sequined cocktail dress was now onstage. I could see her, but I couldn't follow what was going on—not at this moment, not through the remainder of the performance. I was numb with exhilaration.

Following the show, we danced straight through to last call, pumping our arms and hips to the rhythm of the music, our shirts drenched with sweat. I'd never felt so loose, so thrillingly light-headed. Miguel, a dancer capable of dramatic spins, joined us occasionally. The few times we took breaks to down quick beers, I shouted inanities over the incessant disco beat—"Do you like it here in Tucson?"—to which Pablo nodded.

My ears buzzed almost painfully when the music finally stopped. As the Jekyll's staff ushered everybody out, the sudden wash of light, filling the building, shrank rather than expanded the dimensions of the bar. We filed into the parking lot. I was grateful for the darkness. When I asked Pablo if he'd follow in his car to my apartment, he turned to Miguel, who made a clucking sound with his tongue. "You be good to my sister!" he commanded.

Pablo walked to the bedside and switched off the floor lamp. I wrapped my arms around him from behind. But he was all business. In a single motion he shucked his jeans and underwear to the floor. Yanking the sheet and bedspread back, he tumbled onto the bed, drawing just the sheet corner across his waist in a triangle, concealing his erection.

I thumped to the mattress edge, tugging at my jeans and socks. I lowered myself, skin to skin, over his outstretched form. I kissed my way slowly down, from forehead to crotch.

Pablo lay all the while inert. But when I took him into my mouth, he held my head, guiding the motion; and coming, rolled onto his side, facing away.

I ran my hand along his back. He lay so still, if I hadn't known better, I'd have guessed he was sleeping. Turning him onto his stomach, using spit as lubricant, I worked my way into him as gently as I could. His sudden intake of breath, his tense body, made it clear he was in pain, but I didn't stop.

I'd had sex with very few men. The first several times, the newness of what was happening made me so delirious—from the shock of beard stubble when we kissed, to the thrill of grasping a hard cock other than my own—I'd experienced the lovemaking in a near-unconscious daze. I'd grown more self-possessed during my first year of graduate school, bringing home, two or three times, young Hispanics from Jekyll's. As my confidence increased, I fell easily into the same general lovemaking pattern my girlfriends and I had found satisfying for years. A pattern so set it took the form of a story, a script, one I'd masturbated to as a boy while reading the pornographic magazines I found in the trash of the men's dorms near my house.

Though the settings varied, the plots of the magazine stories were essentially the same. Following the opening paragraphs in which the couple is brought together, the guy would take over, from the first kiss to removal of the girl's clothes and his, sometimes undertaken with tenderness, sometimes abandon. Even when the girl seduced the guy, he invariably took charge, exploring her body, exciting them both to the inevitable, often mutual, climax. The rhythms of their lovemaking were under his control. A girl's occasional reciprocal move, such as suddenly going down on the guy, might be exciting, but it was only temporary. In this story, the man, who frequently narrated directly—*I*—was the author.

After making love to Pablo, I quickly fell asleep. At some point before dawn, I felt him crawl from bed—to use the bathroom, I supposed. By the time I realized he had dressed, he was out the door.

All the next day I was sick with anxiety. I couldn't eat or concentrate on anything. I alternated between imagining the whole thing smashed, a joke on me, a fumbling clod whom no exquisite boy like Pablo could ever take seriously, and fantasizing about our future, an absurd story in which I would learn to speak Spanish and Pablo would become a university student. We would move in together; Pablo would get to know my friends, my parents; someday we would travel—to Mexico, to visit Pablo's family, and to Europe, to England and Germany, home of my ancestors; my writing would be influenced by our opposite natures, the complications of our cultures.

I slipped into Jekyll's around nine. I paced the bar full-circle, searching every face in the amphitheater. No Pablo, no Miguel, no Geraldo. I downed a beer, and then another, eyeing the entrance. I imagined Pablo dancing with somebody else at another disco. I acknowledged the stupidity of my tidy little narrative of our future, hating myself for being, in what I considered my advanced age, at the mercy of such adolescent intensities.

Miguel walked in alone. He explained quickly that Pablo had been called home to Mexico on a family matter. Geraldo had decided to go along. "Pablo asked me to take good care of you," he added, wrapping an arm around my waist. Then, "You kept my sister out late!"

"Why did he sneak out like that?"

"A girl can't get her beauty rest in somebody else's bed," he proclaimed.

A few drinks along, I couldn't resist engaging in a series of quick, playful kisses, eyes open and giggling. Miguel provided running commentary on every turn in the drag show: "Ooh, look at that, I just love a girl in a tight leather skirt. But honey, if I had that kind of ass. . . ."

After the show, though our touching and conversation grew increasingly sexual, I wasn't in a mood to dance. The night with Pablo, now Miguel's attentions—I needed to leave the bar, to be alone. Miguel suggested we go to a movie the following night.

When I arrived at the apartment Miguel shared with Pablo and Geraldo, he greeted me with a quick peck on the cheek. He poured me a scotch, then led me down a hall to his bedroom, directing me to sit on the corner of the bed. From here, opposite the open bathroom door, I could watch him apply makeup at the built-in vanity. He painted a precise black line across the skin above one eyelash in a single motion. Not satisfied, he wiped it off with cream and applied the line again.

His hands danced with a practiced grace. "Where'd you learn to use makeup?"

"Some things a girl just knows," he said. But as the minutes passed and he showed no sign of nearing an end, I mentioned we'd miss the movie.

"Pour yourself another scotch," Miguel replied.

Finishing a little after eight, Miguel fixed himself a drink and slipped a Grace Jones tape on the stereo. He drew me down beside him on the couch. But when I tried to give him a kiss, at first he turned away. "Now you be a good boy—till later." Then he pulled me toward him, protesting only mildly when I ran my hand inside his shirt. The give-and-take was familiar to me, like the sexual wrestling I'd enjoyed with girlfriends in adolescence. We kissed for a while, sliding in stages to a horizontal position, my fingers fumbling, finally, with his belt buckle. Suddenly Miguel pushed me back and, sitting up straight, pretended to pat his hair into place. "Time for Jekyll's," he announced.

Our lovemaking later that night mirrored my night with Pablo, Miguel turning oddly lifeless after coming himself. This I was not accustomed to. My girlfriends seemed to enjoy sex as much as I did.

That I should take charge, responsible for his pleasure as well as my own, directing the activities in bed as I did those in public places—opening doors, buying drinks: these behaviors I took for granted. "What a fine little man," my favorite aunt would say to me as a boy when I helped her to a chair before holiday dinners. Every time the comment released a surge of pleasure through my body.

I had always assumed with dates a proprietary air, creating around their bodies a field of control I actually visualized. It seemed not only to work but to be expected. In high school I was brought up short only once that I can remember. My date and I had been necking on her doorstep for several minutes, rubbing against each other's crotches while we embraced. When I turned to leave, she made an observation the truth of which struck me ill with guilt: "Whenever you're ready to stop, you pat me on the back, exactly three times, just like you do your dog."

One college girlfriend and I had toyed, as a political state-

Brown Boys

93

ment, with reversing roles in public. But when she'd open doors for me, help me off with my winter coat, order our meals, it was just theater.

On weekend nights I'd meet Miguel at Jekyll's; Pablo would cruise for somebody new or rejoin the man he'd found a night or week before; Geraldo usually remained at a distance with his boyfriend, Mark, a muscular, tall, sandy-haired mechanic who wore cowboy boots and tooled leather belts—a man, Miguel confided, whom Geraldo and Pablo had quarreled over the night I met them all in Jekyll's. And during these weeks, which spanned most of the summer, Miguel refused to meet my friends. Twice he failed to show up for dinners. "Who wants to meet straight people?" he said.

Not once did we go together to a movie or restaurant or concert. If he agreed to go somewhere other than the bar, he'd delay when I came to pick him up, or arrive late if he was to drive, or simply not show up at all.

Each time my anger dissolved in his presence—the dazzling eyes, quick humor, and, when in the bar, the kissing. My body would flood with desire. He'd call me his husband, a term that always startled me. What pleasure we took in sex we seemed to take alone, though both were necessary to accomplish it.

I had no idea why this was happening. Miguel was all that I could hope for, his androgynous beauty, his obvious intelligence, his foreign otherness that I would someday, somehow, come to know—as he would come to know mine.

As a new graduate student in a small writing program, I had quickly made two friends, a young poet on the faculty and his wife, an artist. Steve's unnerving humor punctured my natural reserve. "Does your mother enjoy sex?" he asked on one of our first evenings out together. After he and Gail taught me to play pinochle, my life changed dramatically. We started playing cards together nearly every weekday night at their dining table. Something beyond shared interests, something fundamental in our habits of mind and heart, brought us into a sudden familial relation to one another. We loved discussing our daily lives and telling our personal stories—about friends, parents, movies we saw or books we read, local politics, dreams we had the night before, and on and on. Their warmth and good humor made an immediate home for me in Tucson. A day without at least a few hours with them was an empty day for me, a lost opportunity.

On weekends before heading to Jekyll's, often I'd have an early drink with these new friends. We'd meet at a slightly grungy bar near campus, The Shanty. A mix of artists, junkies, cowboys, and street people gathered there. (I loved how the hunky bouncer, seated just inside the door, read Tarzan novels by the light of a cigarette machine.) Around nine o'clock, I'd say good night, and Steve and Gail would wish me luck. Sometimes we even visited Jekyll's together. They enjoyed the drag shows, and we had a great time dancing, in pairs or as a threesome. On the occasions I had a date, though, I discouraged them from coming. A noisy gay bar was not a place for them to meet my boyfriends. Too much sexual energy in the air, I told myself.

As the end of summer approached and Miguel prepared for a trip home to Madera, his increasing boredom grew obvious. We were spending more nights together now. I had a three-week break between summer school and the fall semester; Steve and Gail were away on vacation. But Miguel's mood often turned sour at the bar. I experienced a terrible wave of panic the few times he said he wasn't feeling well enough for us to go home together.

I still believed we could break through to some kind of intimacy, which increasingly meant an engagement with the nonerotic sides of our lives. I had given up thinking sex was where two men might discover, might develop, some deeper connection. I longed for the kinds of conversations I had with friends. I longed for the intensity I observed between Steve and Gail. If I brought up matters of family or religion or politics, Miguel would tease me for being too serious. Mostly we talked—gossiped—about the various bar characters we came to know. When I proposed we take a weekend trip together—drive the hundred miles north to Phoenix, where we could rent a hotel room, visit the gay bars by night and my parents by day—a snort of derisive laughter erupted from him.

One night a few days before his trip, Miguel seemed to have regained his spirits. A little giddy, his voice rising and falling with exaggerated drama, he introduced me to William, his "stepsister." A youth about Miguel's height, he had unusually fine, nearly white hair and pale blue eyes. He wore a baggy white polo shirt tucked into very short, tight, ragged Levi's cutoffs, with no underwear: when he perched on a barstool, the head of his penis poked out one side, his scrotum the other.

"You two boys get to know each other while I go make myself beautiful," Miguel said, bouncing off to the bathroom.

I ordered beers. We drank in nervous silence, staring at the bartender as he mixed drinks, made change, wiped the counter.

"So how did you get to know Miguel?" I asked finally.

"We met at the apartment pool. And once we took a trip to San Diego. There's incredible discos there, and a bathhouse with a great orgy room."

I didn't know what to say next.

Miguel came up from behind, placing a hand simultaneously on William's shoulder and mine.

"You never told me about San Diego," I said.

He drew back in mock surprise. "Well, don't get all worked up." He kissed me on the temple. "I loved the bathhouse. And the things I saw in the orgy room! But we both came back with crabs," he laughed.

On he raved about San Diego, about how hot the music was in the discos, about all the beautiful men and how he wanted to move there. As he talked, he grew increasingly animated, gesturing with his hands, touching me, and then William, and then me again, flirting with both of us at once.

Miguel led us onto the dance floor. Early August, most students out of town, we had the floor nearly to ourselves. I reserved most of my eye contact for Miguel. Occasionally I ventured toward William, who liked to dance close.

After a few songs, I slipped away to the bathroom. I watched William and Miguel for a while upon returning. By now they'd pulled off their shirts—two perfectly matched, beautiful young men, one dark, one light.

I unbuttoned my shirt, tugging the tails from my jeans. We danced like this, our chests glistening with sweat, my shirt flapping as I spun, till the DJ dropped the lights all the way down and played the night's only slow song. Collapsing toward one another, we embraced in a circle.

William reached into the top drawer of Miguel's dresser. "I want to see that new movie you got," he said.

Miguel arranged pillows across the headboard while William set up the VCR atop a table at the foot of the bed.

Propped against the pillows, legs outstretched, I sat in the middle as the movie began. It was a silent, amateurish, gay pornographic short. Titled "The Server," it had obviously been shot with a hand-held camera. There were four characters, three blonds and the dark-haired server, who carried a circular tray with drinks. The blonds, in jeans and sport shirts, sat around a patio table next to a kidney-shaped swimming pool. The server wore only a bikini swimsuit. After placing the drinks on the table, the server put his hand on the shoulder of the man closest to him; the man ran his hand up the server's leg, drawing down the swimsuit, out of which popped the server's erect penis. The other couple had started necking and pulling at each other's clothes.

By now William was kissing my neck; Miguel had a hand on my thigh. I could hardly breathe from the pressure of my pounding heart.

We tugged and humped and stumbled over each other's bodies, my attentions generally directed toward Miguel, Miguel's toward William, and William doing his best to expend some energy on both Miguel and me. But I couldn't stay interested with the sudden changes.

The screen was now all flesh, the four men naked, entwined somehow in a single pumping mass near the edge of the pool. Despite the jumpy camera, it seemed as if everything progressed smoothly there.

I slipped out the bedroom door to put my clothes on in the hall, departing without a word.

Miguel was scheduled to leave for Mexico in two days. The next time I saw him, I'd just finished the first week of fall classes. He sat with Geraldo and Mark in the amphitheater of Jekyll's. He nodded, then turned his shoulder to resume conversation. His bland expression, the deliberate turn away, made it clear I had not been invited over. I took a seat at the bar, a little numb. I scanned the crowd mechanically. My eyes stopped at a dark-skinned youth with black curls so shiny they almost looked wet. He wore a tight yellow muscle shirt, which revealed the lift of his pectorals and two tiny nipple peaks.

2

In two years' time I could joke with friends that my address book looked like the Mexican version of one of those pamphlets on what to name the new baby boy: Alfonso, Antonio, Alfredo, Carlos, Fernando, Ignacio, José, Juan, Miguel, Pablo, Pedro, Poncho, Renaldo, Ricardo, Xavier. . . . I'd made a few acquaintances in the bar, Anglos like myself who dated mostly younger Hispanics. We'd had boyfriends in common; it was inevitable we would get to know each other. Sometimes we even flirted with each other's dates. We formed a sort of fraternity, gossiping and making fun of our failures.

One of these acquaintances, Blair, had a wry sense of humor I especially enjoyed. With wavy blond hair and a slight build like mine, he had a subtle speech affectation that made him sound vaguely foreign. At Jekyll's one evening he suggested we become fuck-buddies.

"Fuck-buddies?"

"I had a pal in Houston," he said, "and when we didn't have boyfriends, we'd screw each other, just to take the edge off." I thought he was joking.

A few weeks later, Blair brought the matter up again. He coaxed, flattering me a little. He seemed sophisticated about sex. I'd probably learn something.

In the glow of a corner lamp, Blair's studio apartment reminded me of my own—half of a duplex, a shabby 1930s bungalow with creaky, pitted fir floors and rattly, double-hung windows. I knew without looking that the bathroom sink would be streaked a yellow-brown, the color of chain-smokers' fingers, from a dripping faucet.

I flicked on an overhead light to get a better look around; Blair quickly switched it off, pulling me onto the bed. There was an awkward moment as we each made a move to do a tongue-first inventory of the other's body. I gave in, enjoying this reversal in the ritual. But when I tried to angle myself to go down on Blair, he pushed me back by the shoulders. This made me incredibly dizzy. I was drunker than I thought. Then he urged me over onto my stomach.

Whatever sensations getting screwed might have had for me I could hardly register, though at one point a terrible spasm of pain shot through me. Instead I had to concentrate entirely on not convulsing in a torrent all over the pillow. When Blair rolled away, I ran to the bathroom, vomiting into the toilet.

I returned to the bed feeling terrific, with a great bodily sense of relief and lightness—and horny for my turn. Blair was apparently asleep. I tried to rouse him gently, massaging the muscles at his neck. "*Get away.* Just let me sleep."

I pulled on my clothes. My asshole stung. I felt sick, empty. I felt humiliated.

"Sounds more like a 'fuck you, buddy,'" Barbara said, not looking at me. She was examining the ends of her long, wavy hair. "What are you doing with a white boy, anyway?" She threw the hair back over her shoulder.

Though I'd known her just a week, already I was confiding the most minute details of my sexual life. Barbara had entered the writing program I'd recently completed. Steve had introduced us at a poetry reading. This night we were drinking in The Shanty.

A Polish-American Jew from New York, Barbara combined the street smarts of her working-class neighborhood in Queens with a warmth and ebullience that were immediately winning. And few failed to notice her terrific figure: whether on the way to the disco or the Circle K, she preferred dressing in the miniskirts, net stockings, and low-cut tight blouses of her teenhood. Men trailed in her wake wherever she went, especially bars.

Gay bars, it turned out, she liked best, because of their charged sexual atmosphere. In fact, she loved much about the gay scene, its music and fashion and gender-bending and humor. "I'm a real fagelah hagelah," she said once with a wink—then, impatient with my puzzled look, "Jewish fag hag! Don'tcha get it?"

Brown Boys

100

Barbara teased me endlessly. She found my young Mexican lovers fascinating. She'd needle till she'd gotten every detail about a recent encounter, a particular specialty of hers—everybody seemed to open up to Barbara. When things went badly, she'd exploit some comic angle in the affair, urging me on to the next one. All mixed in was our talk about writing. She could as easily discuss the pros and cons of various lubricants as the sonnets of Robert Lowell.

We started visiting Jekyll's together regularly. Following drag shows, we'd flirt on the dance floor with the guys we found most attractive. Much to my annoyance, she was always better at striking up conversations than I was. Some even invited her home. Once after she'd left me to cruise on my own—I hated approaching anybody with her watching—Pablo walked in. I hadn't seen him in over two years. He and Miguel had made good on their plan to move to San Diego.

The years had wrought astonishing changes in Pablo. His shoulders and upper arms, his chest and neck—his entire upper body—had filled out, firm and muscular. His eyes alone retained their softness. Looking out from the sculptural set of his body, the eyes gave the impression that his former, more boyish self lay trapped beneath the new layers of flesh.

When he embraced me, the embrace was tight and sustained, and he continued to hold me by the waist as we stumbled across our first few sentences. His English was still surprisingly broken. But he didn't want to talk much, especially about his life in San Diego with Miguel. We drank at the bar, mostly in silence, watching the dancers on the disco floor. He had a motel room, he said finally, but would like to spend the night at my apartment. I was intrigued by this new Pablo who was no longer a boy.

Pablo's manner in bed was as transformed as his body. He wrapped his arms around me with obvious desire. He ran his hands down my torso, caressing my hips. He took me briefly into his mouth, then rolled me onto my stomach.

When he pulled away after coming, I tried to draw him to me. He shook his head, curling tight as a fist into the covers. I couldn't get him to continue our lovemaking or even speak to me.

Jumping from the bed, I swept his clothes up in a heap. I threw everything out the apartment door and shoved him into the night.

Then I sat in bed and wept, pulling the bedsheet around me. I knew my anger, my pain, was out of all proportion to what had happened. I knew I should call Barbara, or Steve and Gail. There should be nothing I couldn't tell them, nothing they wouldn't try to help me through. But what I felt was too raw. Something deep within me, at the level of my sense of maleness, was becoming terribly confused, though I couldn't possibly have put it into those terms at the time. I only knew that I couldn't discuss such a feeling with anybody.

3

"Got a light?" The new arrival had walked through the door without breaking stride, negotiating the tables and chairs to a stool at my side as if he could see in the dark.

This sweltering July afternoon, I was drinking in the small back bar of The Stonewall, a bar catering less to students than to working men in their late twenties and thirties. A large fan swept side to side from atop a floor stand in the corner. Every few minutes the door would open, producing a blinding rectangle of yellow. Most newcomers stumbled in, silhouettes groping for a chair-back or steadying table.

I handed the man a matchbook from the counter.

Lighting up, he inhaled deeply, exhaling with obvious relief. "I'm Luis," he said. "Thanks."

He slapped a hand on my thigh. "So tell me all about yourself."

I crossed my arms, part intrigued, part taken aback. "What's to know," I said.

"Maybe all's too much to ask. I'll go first. Sometimes I need a cigarette bad. I'm Luis, but you can call me Margarita." The *r*'s he rolled just slightly. I didn't know how seriously to take that last remark.

His voice was low and gruff. But nothing in his tone, nothing in his forward manner, seemed threatening. And I liked his looks, the disproportion between his wide shoulders and tiny hips; the crinkles around his eyes, his high cheekbones; the thick black hair that fell in waves at his shoulders. I liked especially his crooked, bladey nose.

"Boyer." I offered my hand. Luis's was rough.

"Soft," he said of mine, holding it a moment. He continued to smoke with relish, tilting his head back to exhale, watching each tunnel of smoke swirl to invisibility. "I'll bet you're in business, or a teacher."

"Not exactly. I work at a motel. A dive in South Tucson. I try to keep the hookers out. I'm a desk clerk." I'd been supporting myself this way for several months, my fifth job since graduate school. A three-to-eleven shift, perfect for morning writing, with time left over at night for a drink if I wanted.

"But I did teach once. I'm a writer, a poet." I'm not sure I'd said that last part so soon to a stranger in a bar.

"Well, Mr. Poet, you hear of García Lorca?"

I laughed, uncrossing my arms. "Of course . . . *At five in the afternoon* . . ."—this was all I could remember.

"*A boy brought the white sheet,*" Luis answered. He gave my leg a squeeze. "Let me buy you a beer."

Over the next hour we took turns buying drinks as we talked. Luis lived with friends a mile south of the city, not far from the motel where I worked. His friends employed him as a manager for several properties. He was not Hispanic, he said with playful bravado, or Mexican, or Mexican American. He was Mesquite, which meant half-Apache, half-Mexican, from south Texas. He'd moved to Tucson seven years ago, after a stint in the Navy. They'd booted him for being gay—a fact he'd told them to avoid serving in Vietnam.

The more we talked, the more suggestive our touching became. Luis asked if we could go to my apartment, which was between the bar and his place.

Age twenty-seven, I had grown bone-weary of the patterns I'd fallen into over the past several years. I found it harder to share Barbara's comic perspective. Every few months I'd vow to all my straight friends that I'd given up: no more bars, no more lovers. I'd confess that something in me made it impossible—my controlling nature, my unreasonable expectations. No doubt I was a loner. I'd not made a single enduring friendship in the bars, let alone found a partner.

But always, within a very few weeks, I'd end up missing the company of other gay men. Living in a wholly straight world, whether socializing or at work, I'd begin to feel like an imposter. All my friends were real, themselves; I was just an actor. I'd end up not just horny but craving some form of human connection I had no idea how to achieve—and I'd visit the bars.

In our first week together, I discovered that Luis's friends did in fact call him Margarita—after his favorite drink. His living arrangement reminded me of the Cartwright ranch on TV's *Bonanza*. Around a large central house with high, beamed ceilings and flagstone floors, seven smaller structures circled like planets. Built in the twenties, all were painted brown and had Santa Fe–style *vegas* poking out their front walls. Though two were rented, the rest were occupied by youths whose numbers swelled and shrank like weekly tides.

The young men, teenagers mostly, could live at The Hacienda, as everybody called the property, for as long as they liked, providing they worked. All were gay and all had stories about how the owner and resident overlord, Peter, had helped them. He'd hired a lawyer for one boy whose parents disowned him when he got busted for selling marijuana. Another had hitched to L. A. after his father beat him, having discovered he was gay; Peter wired bus fare back to Tucson when the kid got picked up as a vagrant. At any given time, as many as a dozen such boys lived at The Hacienda. There seemed to be some sort of network that directed them to Peter.

Luis, hardly a boy at thirty-three, revered Peter for a past favor he refused to reveal. He loved him as well for his generosity in taking in so many lost souls. He'd become Peter's business manager, overseeing not only restoration of The Hacienda but Peter's other properties in town. The only other more-or-less permanent characters were Harry, the Hacienda cook, gray-haired and raw-faced (looking much older than the fifty-eight he'd admit to), who drank vodka in a juice glass from breakfast till bedtime, whipping up enormous meals for all the Hacienda inhabitants; and Barry, Peter's lover, in his thirties, pudgy and quarrelsome, like an overgrown baby, who'd been with Peter since he was seventeen.

Peter ruled The Hacienda absolutely, barking orders with obvious delight. Ruddy, his fair skin roughened by exposure to the sun, he was short and compact, in his early fifties. Nobody crossed him— except his favorite, Luis—without serious consequences. And he had a voice, a laugh, that boomed, dominating every conversation. Always intense, he loved to poke fun. Me he instantly dubbed "the Professor."

"So, Professor," he said, as we sat to breakfast following my first night over, "you gonna write poems about my Margarita?"

I shifted in my seat, forcing a laugh. I'd not felt ill at ease in quite this way since high school and the questions I sometimes got from the fathers of dates.

"Be good, Boss," Luis said in a low voice. Standing behind Peter, he placed his hands on the older man's shoulders and kissed the bald spot on his crown.

For the first several weeks, I was convinced that this time things would work out. That Luis was older seemed an important change. And how gratifying to experience some continuity between our public selves and the ones behind bedroom doors. The affection and humor we shared when among Luis's friends charged our sex lives; Luis was a spirited, inventive sexual partner, full of surprises. His manner, his character, was as dynamic as I'd ever experienced. By turns gruff and coy and assertive and tender, he seemed not to "play" himself but to be, wholly, unself-consciously, whoever emerged from the emotions of his current moment. I found myself always slightly off balance in the most pleasant way. We had intense late-night talks about everything, family, sex toys, movie stars, politics, art.

A blending of our social worlds also seemed possible. He appeared, only slightly late, only slightly drunk, for a dinner with Barbara. Not surprisingly, he and Barbara hit it off immediately, talking excitedly throughout the evening. During those first weeks, I even dared to imagine what it would be like for us to live together.

I assumed my mild discomfort when at The Hacienda would wear off once I got to know everybody better. The swirl of boys in and out, their almost universal disconnection from families and society in general, was painful for me to witness. One morning, on my way to the kitchen from Luis's room to get water, I discovered three new boys sprawled in their underwear on the great U-shaped arrangement of couches in the living room. I could never be sure: were the older men sleeping with these boys? Few hung around for long; most seemed dulled by one form of abuse or another. Their lives had been unlike anything I'd known, with one notable exception, my being gay. But this had caused only slight disruption in my family and none in my friendships.

Luis's world was so alien that I tried to come to know it as I might an uncaptioned foreign film: by trusting that the story's shape would eventually make itself known, if I remained alert.

Peter made me most uncomfortable of all. Unlike the boys, I owed him nothing. Yet the force of his character intimidated me. I hardly spoke in his presence, especially when he was in a joking mood. Luis was usually able to cover, taking up Peter's challenge whenever he turned his attention to me. They both seemed to enjoy these verbal contests, even if Luis did sometimes push too far. Comments about Barry, an easy target, could touch a nerve. Barry avoided the group, often retreating to the room he shared with Peter.

My silence quickly became one of Peter's favorite subjects. "The Professor is feeling deep tonight," he said once as we drank at a restaurant bar, waiting for our table. "A boilermaker for your thoughts." He pushed his own untouched whiskey and beer-back over to me.

"His thoughts aren't *all* that goes deep," Luis parried, drawing me toward him by the neck.

Sexual innuendo was the quickest way out of difficult moments with Peter. To get along, I'd pretend to flirt. Peter would nuzzle my ear or rub up against my crotch. He'd needle Luis. "Better watch out, Margarita, I think I'm in love with your fiancée."

Peter frequently used language of this sort—of marriage, husband and wife; of who was top, who bottom—when referring to me and Luis. A few years before, such language half amused me; increasingly I sensed too little irony in its use by the gay men I hung out with. The inherent put-down of the one who was bottom gnawed at me. We were all men. It shouldn't matter whether we took pleasure in being top, bottom, or sideways.

Luis was an expert at such banter. He brushed off my suggestion that such terms might have sexist implications. "Lighten up," he said repeatedly, "I'll make you a good wife."

I came to dread mornings at The Hacienda when we'd all gather for breakfast, as well as weekend nights in the bars. I came to dread the public gestures of control and dependence, so carefully monitored by everyone in our group, including me: who opened doors for whom, who sat on whose lap, who embraced whom from behind at the kitchen sink or on the dance floor. The more I thought of myself as a gay man the past few years, the deeper my discomfort whenever I undertook these rituals I'd practiced in my young adulthood with girlfriends. I recognized something dehumanizing in the equations—an obvious projection of sexism onto the relations among gay men. Surely being gay meant *not* recreating straight attitudes and behavior.

Still I couldn't rise above it all. I'd experience an inner sinking whenever Peter made gestures placing me in the "girl's" position, whenever he made a show of opening a door for me or paying for my meal.

Luis seemed to do little better when out with my friends. At The Shanty or a party at Steve and Gail's, he became someone I only partly recognized. Polite, almost courtly, he was drained of his characteristic exuberance, cautious of any but the most incidental forms of touching. We were comfortable together—we were ourselves—only when alone. Privacy freed us of whatever made us not fit inside our own skins in public settings.

Over a four-month period, Luis grew querulous as I declined more and more often to spend nights at The Hacienda. When I suggested we try living together in my apartment, that this might enable us to work things out, he countered that I should move in with *him* and become part of *his* family. One evening, in a narrow, dark bar generally considered a hangout for older gay men—that is, men in their thirties and forties—I rose to excuse myself as The Hacienda group discussed where to go for dinner.

Luis shoved himself back from the table. "Motherfucker-
motherfuckermother . . . ," he motored under his breath, hauling me
out of the bar.

I didn't resist. I had a pretty good idea of what he was about
to say: *I could go fuck myself if his friends weren't good enough.
What the hell was wrong with me?*

I stood frozen at first. What *was* wrong with me? Unable to
speak, I tried to embrace him. He shoved me back, whirling to slam
through the bar door.

The next day I sent him a dozen long-stem red roses with an
invitation to dinner. By the time he arrived at my apartment, I'd
downed several beers. He'd been drinking too. We embraced, pulling at each other's clothes, making love with an almost angry intensity. Then Luis dressed and drove away for the last time.

4

Shortly after the affair with Luis, I made a new friend, my first gay
friend. That is, I began my first serious, nonsexual relationship with
another gay man. Barbara introduced me to him. He was a writer, a
new graduate student, on the lookout for a cheap place to live. As
luck would have it, the apartment adjoining mine was available.

In long talks on the patio we shared, we narrated our lives,
the way people often do when striking up new friendships. Patrick's
stories I found fascinating—and refreshing. Having known he was
gay from an early age, from at least the time of his first childhood
lover, he seemed to have an utterly open-eyed understanding of his
own sexuality. One image in particular has lodged in my memory
from those conversations nearly twenty years ago: Patrick and that
first boyfriend entwined on a grassy hill beside a river, a sailboat
passing by, the people on board waving, the boys waving back.

Shaping my stories aloud, having a gay listener, a skilled
story-maker, helped me to consider implications I'd not been able

to articulate alone or with straight friends. I now had to face the obvious. I couldn't ignore the racist overtones to my obsession with these boys. Clearly the young men I'd been dating the past five years made convenient stand-ins for the girls of my youth. I'd simply transferred the behaviors and expectations, many betraying sexist attitudes, from my earlier life to my relations with my first gay lovers. My instinctive attractions had been little more than an unconscious attempt to recreate the familiar.

I confess I am as uncomfortable today at forty-seven as I was in my late twenties with such explanations, not only because they expose in me attitudes I abhor. They reduce so terribly the complexity, the richness, of my felt experience; they reduce so terribly the mystery and vitality of those mutual attractions.

Nevertheless, the more I observed the romantic relations of other gay men from this perspective, the more I could see the problem as basic to our struggles to attain authentic gay identities. Over and over, I could hear the same unspoken question behind the tensions I witnessed between lovers, especially couples of my generation or older: *who gets to be the man?* Both can't be male, nor can both share equally in the making of the relationship if the model, unconscious or otherwise, is heterosexual and sexist.

On my own I had sensed for some time that I was attempting to live somebody else's story. Now that I had some knowledge of the story's sources, I still had no idea how to begin a new one. Following the breakup with Luis, all I could think to do was practice crude denial. I'd simply deny what still felt like instinctive desires—ignore my attraction to younger Hispanics. I'd force myself to look elsewhere, just to see where it might lead.

I gained an increment of self-awareness almost immediately. I could be in nearly any public setting—shopping at a mall or supermarket, walking on the university campus to a poetry reading, standing in a movie theater lobby—when I'd discover my eyes focused on a dark young man. Already I had stared the extra instant that, if the youth were also gay, would signal my interest. I've never known a gay man who didn't learn to identify other gay men in just this way, a practice that develops with no formal training necessary. And straight men hardly ever notice.

My resolve to break old patterns didn't help at first. No matter that, when visiting gay bars, I'd walk through the door focused on meeting a different kind of man. Within minutes my gaze would settle automatically on a dark-skinned youth.

Each time this happened I'd lower my eyes, wondering how anything so deeply embedded could ever be overcome. Then I'd command myself to search for an older face, lighter in color, more like my own. If I discovered someone who looked intriguing, I'd study his face, his posture, the line of his shoulders, waist, hips. Was there anything intrinsically undesirable in these features?

Sometimes my look was returned. My insides churning, I'd do my best to strike up a conversation. If we were able to talk comfortably, if I sensed a mutual interest, if we went so far as to dance a little, agreeing to meet again, I'd struggle to imagine *no* particular future with this one. Since the story I'd grown up with had failed me, I'd enter the next day, and then the next, maintaining as best I could a faith in a need for *no* story, maintaining an openness to whatever might come.

The going was often rough. At first I found the discomfort of letting go of expectation nearly unbearable—the hope of a settled, domestic relationship, and the heterosexual scripts: *who gets to be the man?* I blundered many times, making assumptions, pushing a new romantic interest to define in narrow ways what I vowed I no longer wanted defined: who we were to one another, and where we might be headed. Guys looking for a little good sex couldn't believe their bad luck in stumbling on such a serious trick.

Several times when all the external pieces seemed in place— our personalities, ages, range of interests—I'd will myself into a sexual relationship though I felt no desire for the man. Desire would

come later, I'd rationalize; our erotic life would grow from everything else we shared. Lasting a month or more, at best such affairs
produced a kinship at the level of fuck-buddies. Like choosing your
brother for a lover.

More important, suspending such personal story-making was
profoundly alien to my nature. To have a story is to have a meaning;
a writer is a meaning-maker. How could I not search for meaning in
each unfolding moment?

Much to my surprise, I did get better at it over the ensuing
months. I practiced with friends, especially Patrick, repeating like a
mantra, *We have no future, we have no future, and it doesn't matter,*
about some potential boyfriend. I found in time that not having
or assuming a story also produced an oddly pleasant sensation, a
sensation analogous to the tension I experience in the first stages
of working on a new poem: underlying the broad wash of uncertainty—*this will never amount to anything*—an energizing sense of
limitless potential—*this could be the breakthrough to a new kind of
understanding.*

During the three years leading to my thirtieth birthday, in ad-
dition to several brief affairs, I entered into two more extended relationships, both with men about my age. What seemed to give these
relationships greater vitality was our self-confessed uncertainty—
and the subsequent care we took in coming to know one another.
The dynamics of our sexual selves we worked out slowly, if somewhat awkwardly, neither of us attempting to define himself or the
other through the complications, the mysteries and pleasures, of
making love. We were able to acknowledge we didn't understand
exactly what was going on. *Who gets to be the man?* grew increasingly irrelevant, replaced by *who am I really, now that I'm with you?*
Both men had experienced the grip of sexual obsessions analogous
to my own. Given all the strangeness and inner turmoil of our twenties, we felt we'd survived a second adolescence: in place of disrup-

tive hormones, unconscious attitudes had been released into our blood—and we were working them out of our systems.

I've struggled almost two decades with the process of suspending my need for a defining narrative. Fifteen years I've shared the struggle with the same man, twelve under the same roof. When I first met him, I discovered that he, as if by instinct, distrusted any hint of a narrative imposed on his life—particularly by me. Who could know his intentions and inner thoughts? He remains one of the most intensely private people I've ever met.

In our early years, while seeing other men, we came to know one another in fits and starts. He'd sometimes disappear for days at a time. Was he out of town, or simply refusing to answer the phone, to come to the door when I knocked? Usually I'd tie these disappearances to things I'd said when we were with friends. "We were thinking we might like to . . ." or "We found the movie to be somewhat. . . ." Surely I'd seen him bristle at my choice of pronoun. I could never be sure. Occasionally he announced his return by leaving flowers from his garden, anemones or sweet peas, in a jar on my doorstep.

One of his closest friends had a story for him, a common enough story, which she confided one night in a bar: he's a loner, she said; if I hoped in any way to be his partner, I must understand I would never live with him. It took me days to absorb the sting of that pronouncement. I tried to imagine how we might share a life while occupying separate houses. Soon after accepting that this might be possible, I sat in shock on my living room couch: we should unhook ourselves from the too-settled patterns of our lives, he said; we should try living together.

Ironically, the weddings of several close friends during these years helped reinforce my thinking about how to go forward. At each wedding ceremony, I found myself moved to tears by the familial and religious benedictions offered the couple, the new husband and wife. Expectation for the roles they would fulfill, and their place in the community order, embraced them, embraced us all like a warming ether.

I participated in that expectation, though surely no such public benedictions would ever accompany my life commitment to another man, should I choose to make one. Yet at some point while celebrating with the wedding party, I experienced an overwhelming relief, relief that this was so. With that wave of glad emotion I could breathe deeply again. I realized I'd felt, till that moment, constrained, as if reduced to very short breaths. Having come this far, how much easier to know, if not to accomplish, the task of fashioning, with another, freshly, on a daily basis, a narrative. How much easier to resist shaping that narrative on the old stories, so that we might share an authoring of our identities. Surely this is what two people must do if they would live in a state of intimacy.

Reading the Body

Across from me sits a dark-haired young man, perhaps seventeen, whose plain round face is marked by a mild outbreak of acne. His eyes, large and brown, pass over me easily, then out the train window, as I settle into my seat. His clothes strike me as charmingly typical for his age: stone-washed jeans, a dark blue T-shirt emblazoned with a KISS EUROTOUR logo beneath an unzipped, eye-stopping windbreaker—a patchwork of neon-bright chartreuse and pink and orange. On one knee rests his daypack, well worn at the seams.

I can't help cataloging his every ordinary detail—and smiling at the lesson in his plainness. I realize I'd fantasized, like a dreamy adolescent, that the men on this trip would approximate the beautiful Italian characters I've seen so often in movies—the self-absorbed Gino, for example, in the recent *Where Angels Fear to Tread*, his nose and cheeks and chin as finely chiseled as a fifth-century sculpture; his chest, in billowy, unbuttoned satin shirts or shirtless altogether, a flawless mahogany.

My partner and I, a painter and a poet, Arizona natives, are remarkably untraveled, given our love of art and our ages. At forty, I've visited exactly three cities beyond the U.S. borders: Nogales, Mexico, sixty-five miles south of Tucson, where we live; Toronto; and Montreal. Gary, who is forty-five, traveled twenty years ago in Mexico.

This June day, however, we are on a train running southeast through the Po Valley from Milan to Bologna. For what seems an eternity, we have been in planes, on shuttle buses, in air and train terminals, and finally in this second-class train car. We've folded ourselves into the cramped seats of public conveyances (or waited to fold ourselves into them) for over eighteen hours; we've been awake for more than twenty. Yet now, at least for me, everything delights, the pimply young man, the four-year-old boy next to him who tugs with his teeth at the ham in his hard-roll sandwich, the mother who seated the boy there, who eyes him solicitously from across the aisle, giving little hand signals to direct his lunch excavations—everything delights, now that I am in Italy.

Gary stares out the train window, his face relaxed, at the moment unreadable. I would guess he's struck by the greens that stretch in endless variety to the horizon—crops, fields of corn and grape arbors for miles, with here and there patches, like lovely rashes, of wild red poppies. Six-foot-two, with square, wide shoulders and narrow hips, he is ropy and dust dry. From long hours outdoors—a love of solitary work in the garden and solitary hiking—his skin is cooked dark; his face, when he laughs, crinkles endlessly. This face I have learned to study to consider what he might be thinking; he says little, and dislikes, especially, me speaking for him.

As for myself, I can hardly sit still for the thrum of adrenaline. In this mood, not unlike the cell-to-cell heightening of sensation I used to experience in the early days of a new sexual love, every image seems to bear special significance.

Now the young man seated across from me turns to the boy, then winks and chucks the boy's chin, tousling his hair. I'm momentarily startled. The boy kicks both his legs joyfully and grins all round. Heads pop out across the aisle, the mother and passengers in our area a fleet of smiles. To touch a stranger's child—as an American, I'm trained against such familiarity; as a homosexual, I find the injunction raised to the level of taboo.

The tableau evaporates quickly as we settle into our separateness, the boy having at his sandwich, the young man gazing out the window again, his knees, spread wide apart, bobbing at intervals with the train's motion. I cross my legs, for some reason feeling a need to cover myself. Gary shifts—he never quite fits in train or plane seats, his shoulders too wide, legs too long; he opens the guidebook on his lap. And then I think I see the young man massaging his crotch, stroking himself up and down with the fingers of his right hand, slowly, giving at last a little squeeze.

Amused, not quite believing, I watch this from the edge of my vision while smiling toward the child. Next the youth absentmindedly tugs at the daypack drawstring draped over his thigh, pulling it taut between his legs. With his left hand, he runs the button on this string rhythmically, faster and faster, up and down its length, five or six inches.

~

Bologna, famous for its centuries-old university, is renowned as well for the two medieval towers still standing side by side in the city's old quarter. We know this not only from reading our guidebook but from comments by the couple who will be our hosts in Italy. Michelle, for many years one of Gary's closest Tucson friends, and her fiancé, Riccardo, a native Bolognan who visits us often, have frequently mentioned the visual drama and delight of Le Due Torre.

So it comes as no surprise, shortly after we drop our luggage in the foyer of our friends' apartment, when they urge an evening stroll before dinner to the towers, Garisenda and Asinelli. From there, Riccardo assures us, it's just a short walk to the Piazza Maggiore, Bologna's central square—where, if we're not too tired, we might stop for a drink at one of the bar-cafes.

Though Gary and I have been up now for more than a day, our friends' enthusiasm and the cool evening air, sweeping through the third-floor apartment from balcony doors off the kitchen, give

us new life. Besides, we both feel a powerful need to stretch our
legs after the long confinement of travel.

Garisenda and Asinelli pop into view in just a few short
blocks—as soon as we step from the covered sidewalk. Instantly Riccardo slips into a more confident, almost textbook prose. (At other
times, he hesitates, groping for the right word, having spoken English for only three years; perhaps he's practiced these phrases with
other Tucson travelers—we're the third set to visit him in the last six
months.)

"In the Middle Ages, there were towers like these all over
Italy," he begins, the fingers of his right hand uncoiling to emphasize the point. "But ours are in especially good condition." By his
tone, one can tell he has sincere affection for the landmarks.

Michelle, who holds on to Riccardo's arm up near the shoulder,
points out her favorite architectural details as we walk: frescoed ceilings of upper apartments, glimpsed through windows whose shut-
ters have been thrown open to the night; ornate marble inlays in
building foyers; tall carved entry doors with brass door-knockers
cast as small lions' heads or small hands. Since May, she and
Riccardo have strolled this way almost every evening, she says.

The stark, four-sided towers, meanwhile, rise ever higher, like
cubist missiles, as we draw nearer. At more than three hundred feet,
Asinelli is particularly commanding; Garisenda, half as tall, tilts
drunkenly to one side.

"Wealthy families were always at war with each other; the
towers were their forts," Riccardo explains.

Mixing my centuries, I immediately imagine the nobles I've
seen in Renaissance paintings—the gentlemen in their velvet gar-
ments and embroidered tunics, the bejeweled ladies in puffy satin
gowns—huffing up narrow, twisting staircases at a moment's notice.

"At one time we had over two hundred towers." Riccardo
sweeps his hand toward the night sky proudly. "All over Europe,
Bologna was known as Turrita, City of Towers."

It occurs to me that, here in the presence of only two, their singularity, their unique *scale,* lends them majesty now—if not a touch of phallic absurdity.

"And the bigger the better," Riccardo adds. "Every man wanted a bigger one than his neighbors."

"Some things never change," Michelle intones, as if reading my mind, her voice low in mock seriousness.

"What?" Riccardo eyes us.

"Every man wanted a bigger one . . . ," she repeats.

"Sure!" Riccardo's face lights in a broad smile. "That too!" Even his forehead plays a role, the brow wrinkling as his eyebrows jump. Gary just shakes his head.

A block further on, the Piazza Maggiore opens out before us. Its sudden airy volume, after the mile of narrow streets we've wandered, is stunning. I take in a deep, involuntary breath. And then I see why the piazza's expanse is so striking. Light from strategically placed floodlights splashes the facades of grand Gothic and Renaissance buildings on all four sides, up massive stone columns, across bas-relief figures and patterned, ornamental shapes. Opposite from where we stand, the never-completed Basilica di San Petronio is particularly impressive for its contrasts: on the lower half, horizontal bands of red and white marble, richly carved; above, rising a hundred feet, nothing but plain, raw brickwork, looking much like the exposed adobe of Spanish missions in the Sonoran Desert. The whole piazza, lit at its edges, glows with an exquisite unreality, reminding me of so many Fellini night scenes.

When I am able to look ground-level, I see small groups of people sitting in broken rows along the basilica steps and strollers crossing this way and that at angles, one couple walking arm in arm, a giant schnauzer at their side. My insides hum with the thrill of it all, yet I experience no urge to rush my step. The rhythm of the piazza is obviously leisurely, a rhythm I fall into gratefully.

We stumble in one direction, then another. We want to see

Reading the Body

everything, from the high, ornamented arches of second-story windows along the east side (Renaissance apartments for university faculty), to Giambologna's three-tiered, sixteenth-century fountain of Neptune, who towers above the level of the piazza at the north-west entrance.

We spend a long time gathering in all the details, all the nuance, of this fountain. Though a bundle of muscle, Neptune strikes me as more a welcoming figure than a fearful one. His posture is soft, almost sensual, his right knee bent, the foot resting on a dolphin in sinuous motion. As in most Neptune sculptures, his right hand supports the trident; but in this one he grasps it low on the pole behind his shoulder, his arm swung back at a gentle angle like a relay runner reaching for a baton. His left leg, bearing the weight of the body, tilts slightly, pushing the hip forward. And his left arm he extends toward the square as a balance to the right while gazing over his left shoulder.

One perspective we most certainly would have missed had not Riccardo, grinning slyly, nudged us into the perfect spot to appreciate the sculptor's humor. Guiding each of us in turn by the shoulders, he has us stand just back of Neptune's right hip. All we can see, looking up, of the god's extended left arm, which is shielded by his torso, is the tip of his thumb—like the head of a dauntingly long and erect penis.

Seated, finally, at an outdoor cafe table directly across the piazza from the Basilica di San Petronio, whose lighted upper expanse stretches, flat and broad—as if an enormous human brow towers opposite us—I have to give up on the conversation running among Michelle, Gary, and Riccardo. The mix of exhilaration, fatigue, and pleasant alienation I feel in this new time and place, thirty hours from another life, one I can hardly seem to remember, leaves me numb.

Michelle and Gary talk excitedly about possibilities for tomorrow. I love seeing him so voluble. Michelle, whom he cares for deeply (a psychic once told him she'd been his sister in a former life), can draw him out like nobody else. She throws her long black hair back from her shoulder, laughing at something he has said. Then Riccardo points to something in the middle of the piazza.

I stare blankly at our drinks. I think I have never seen a more beautiful green than the green of the mysterious aperitif Riccardo has ordered for us; standing in four tall, narrow, inverted glass bells on stems, they glow as if lit from within on the perfectly white tablecloth.

~

I've not trusted my own eyes ever since the youth on the Po Valley train. Gary also noticed him, I discover when I bring up the subject late that night (as we fit sheets to the foldaway bed in Riccardo and Michelle's living room); he too thought the young man's actions oddly, if unconsciously, sexual. But I've not had the nerve to mention that I think I notice men everywhere touching themselves in public. The whole thing seems a little silly. I can't stop myself, however, from keeping count.

In Florence, our third day in Italy, we visit the Uffizi, the museum housing the Medici art collection. I stand in tears before the Botticelli *Annunciation*. Something in the purity of Mary's isolation, the indeterminacy of her gaze—if she looks anywhere, it must be inward. Each object in the narrative is rendered with a radiant precision, the artist's care a form of love, from Gabriel's transparent outer garment to the pale gray-and-green-checkered marble floor tiles beneath Mary's feet. The exquisite stillness of the moment I find wrenchingly beautiful. Botticelli seems unconcerned with showing the world what he can do with paint; rather, he draws all attention to the nature of the moment; he embodies, and the viewer experiences, the poignancy of Mary's fate.

After four hours in the museum, we stroll across the Ponte Vecchio, the bridge where Dante first caught sight of Beatrice, through the courtyard of the Pitti Palace to the grounds of the Boboli Gardens, the gardens of the Medicis. Dazed by so many medieval and Renaissance masterpieces, I'm grateful for this resting place, the acres of cool tree-lined paths, the grace of fountains, the views of Florence from hilltop lookouts. A more extraordinary day is unimaginable.

Yet on the train from Bologna to Florence, in walks from the Duomo to the Uffizi, from the Uffizi across the Ponte Vecchio to the gardens and back, and on the train home to Bologna again, I cannot stop myself from registering eleven touches. And on our second evening walk to the Piazza Maggiore, five more. And on the day we stand speechless inside the Scrovegni Chapel in Padua, a day-trip by train—Giotto's frescoes, the modeling of human features and swirls of grieving angels a mystery of beauty I fumble to express in my journal, the pages an abstract expressionist tangle of scrawled phrases and blacked-out words, the frescoes, I decide, a mystery of beauty no prose can embody—nine more touches.

"Michelle," I say our fourth day at breakfast, a roll and *caffe con latte* with two spoons of sugar—I'm hooked, me, who for years insisted self-righteously it's not coffee if you put something in it—"do men here...." I lose my nerve. Then find it again: "Do men here ... *touch* themselves in public?"

"Yeeeeees," she yowls, stretching the word interminably, her pitch ascending. "Riccardo, did you hear that?"

He smiles weakly. Down. At his roll.

"They do it all the time! Anywhere!" Syllable by syllable, her pitch streaks up and down. "On all his jeans, he's got this little worn spot," she says, staring at Riccardo, who won't meet her eyes. "It drives me crazy when I do the laundry."

⌇

We have been in Italy less than a week, yet a curious—and wholly unanticipated—theme has crept into my journal. I determine to discuss it with Gary as I sit alone on the steps of the Duomo in Florence at the end of our second day-trip here, a day we devote primarily to the art in churches.

Dusk, the square between the Duomo and the Baptistry is a great outdoor theater with many stages, small dramas taking place everywhere. A group of sailors dressed in identical white uniforms, topped by white berets with black tassels, stand side by side, arms looped shoulder over shoulder, a chorus line. In their vertical regularity they remind me of the folds of an accordion. They've asked a young woman in red Lycra pants and halter top, her dark hair hanging to her waist, to take eight snapshots, one for each of them.

Behind these sailors, groups gather and disperse at intervals before the magnificent Ghiberti bronze door of the Bapistry, which depicts Old Testament stories: a tall, middle-aged woman in a severe blue suit addresses a dozen schoolgirls, who listen with admirable concentration as she gestures from one narrative panel to the next; then a young woman in leopard-patterned miniskirt and black high heels poses, one foot perched on the second bar of the protective railing, while her female companion snaps photos from a variety of angles; next, seven elderly couples, all wearing sneakers, approach.

What draws my attention from them—and convinces me to discuss with Gary my journal observations—are the antics of four teenagers, two boys and two girls, not twenty feet in front of the step on which I sit. The two boys seem to be flirting with the girls by being sexual with one another. They wrap their arms around each other's waists; one lays his head on his friend's shoulder. The girls burst into laughter. The boys draw apart, pretending their feelings are hurt. Then one gives the other a kiss on the cheek. The girls double over, jerk up, briefly turn their backs, swing around, their hands at their mouths, a twist of giggles. Now the boys are laughing, their pose exposed. Then the taller wraps himself around his shorter friend from behind, resting his chin on the boy's shoulder.

This goes on and on, the boys doing anything they can to keep the girls entertained, riding piggyback, holding hands, blowing in each other's ears. Their play is a dance, spontaneous and graceful, not the least like the boyish roughhousing I remember from my youth—also performed at times in front of girls to impress. These boys *do* know how to touch each other's bodies.

I'm fascinated, and frustrated Gary has been gone the whole time, circling the Duomo for twilight photos. During the thirty minutes he's been away, the square has vibrated with youthful energy, not only the four I've been watching closely, but two boys and a girl on scooters playing tag, zagging this way and that, half a dozen dark-haired young men dressed like *New York Magazine* models, pleated pants and bright, billowy shirts with slicked hair, who stride off and onto the square (though where they go off to I can't tell), as well as an indeterminate number of young people in groups and solo on the steps around me and in the open area that I don't bother to follow, not wanting to miss the next move by the flirting boys.

Shortly after Gary rejoins me, as I'm trying to fill him in on the various scenes, two motorcycle officers zip to a halt at the edge of the square. Instantly the hum and weave of youths evaporates. The space stands two-thirds empty, stripped to those of us who are middle-aged or older and one young woman with a baby in a stroller.

Reading the Body

124

I have a memory that is kin to this feeling, this undercurrent I've been experiencing. As an adolescent twenty-five years ago, confused by my sexual fantasies about other boys, I was moved inexplicably by certain stories. Thomas Mann's *Death in Venice* especially I remember reading with a fascination that entered my body as a physical sensation. This was something other, something beyond the usual pleasure of entering the lives of compelling fictional characters. A part of me was being addressed that I didn't yet know myself how to contact.

> [T]he boy was absolutely beautiful. His face, pale and reserved, framed with honey-colored hair, the straight sloping nose, the lovely mouth, the expression of sweet and godlike seriousness, recalled Greek sculpture of the noblest period; and the complete purity of the forms was accompanied by such a rare personal charm that, as [Aschenbach] watched, he felt that he had never met with anything equally felicitous in nature or the plastic arts.

I'd read nothing quite like this open adoration of a boy's features. At this point Aschenbach tells himself his interest in Tadzio is aesthetic; by midstory an element of eroticism infuses his descriptions:

> His honey-colored hair clung in rings about his neck and temples. The sun made the down on his back glitter; the fine etching of the ribs, the symmetry of the chest, were emphasized by the tightness of the suit across the buttocks.

On the steps of the Florence Duomo, I confess to Gary having experienced Tadzios everywhere, not just boys but men and girls and women so striking that in their form and motion I think I see a synthesis of the aesthetic and the sensual. At the Uffizi two days earlier, in the Botticelli Room, as I leaned to note the delicacy of detail in the flowers at the lower left corner of *Primavera*, I caught sight of an extraordinary family standing to my side—two boys, a girl, their mother, all with wavy golden hair, satin skin, perfect oval faces, and oversized soft eyes. They might have stepped from a Bot-

Reading the Body

ticelli canvas. That day they seemed to follow us—to the Boboli
Gardens, then the Masaccio frescoes, and finally the train station.

But it wasn't just their physical beauty that moved me. I was
transfixed by their ongoing physical relation to one another, the
way the siblings and mother brushed or leaned unconsciously on
each other's bodies, holding hands loosely, sometimes by one or
two fingers, releasing their contact and then reconnecting as easily
as breathing. These touches were not claims, not the nudges, the
protective, confining embraces, that tell a child or sibling that somebody else is in charge. The family, rather, seemed wrapped in an
invisible, blanketing dance of comfort.

As my emotion grows in the telling, Gary simply nods in ac-
knowledgment. I am always more excitable, more effusive, than he
is. I'm relieved he at least remembers the family.

The men and boys are what most amaze me, I confide, given
the taboo I grew up with against men touching. I find my days here
infused—I'm almost ashamed to say it—with a heightened sensuality. (What I don't say—it's the kind of thing we don't know how to
discuss, and who wants to break the spell?—what I don't say is that
I sense in our lovemaking, since we got to Italy, a new intensity.)

I recount how often I've seen men in unself-conscious contact with each other's bodies. In the central shopping district of
Bologna, how often pairs, many of whom I take to be fathers and
sons, walk arm in arm. One twosome wore similar dark suits and
ties, their resemblance startling, the round faces, slightly down-
turned noses, and small, close-set dark eyes; the father a shrunken,
silver-haired version of the black-haired, thirtyish man attached to
his side.

And on the train back from Padua, how the schoolboys stood
in bunches, draped on one another, at times virtually entwined for
balance in the aisles, joking and singing songs, bursting with adrenaline, unable to remain seated. At train stations their voices soared

as they hung out the car windows. At one stop, a boy standing next to my seat raced to the end of the car. I watched as he threw his arms around a young man who had just climbed aboard. Startled at first, the new passenger, recognizing his assailant, embraced him tightly, face flushed. They kissed, pulled back, embraced again and kissed again, speaking both at once and rapidly. And then they separated, heading in opposite directions.

Almost daily in Italy, in the presence of certain works by Giotto, Fra Angelico, Masaccio, Filippino Lippi, Botticelli, Piero della Francesca, I have been deeply stirred as I am each time I hear the simple, haunting theme and harmonic progression underlying the Allegretto of Beethoven's Symphony No. 7; as I am each time I watch, in the closing moments of the film *Babbette's Feast,* the old worshipers joining hands round the wishing well, following their transforming encounter with sensuality, with God's healing grace.

I can't help fumbling to name these sensations, these moments of body knowledge; Gary can't help remaining silent, at home in color and line and volume as means of conveying the unutterable.

The body knowledge we experience through art, we *do* work in our own ways to negotiate; body knowledge of the erotic or sexual in our daily lives, on the other hand, we are spectacularly incapable of articulating. In these matters our understanding accrues through action over the years. We dare not speak of what we feel, let alone talk about what we do—as though mysteries of the flesh are too powerful, too interior, to enter into through language. My small confession on the steps of the Florence Duomo is as close as I can usually come to discussion of such subjects.

This time it is enough. On the train back to Bologna, a young man in our compartment lounges, half asleep, head resting on a male friend's shoulder, their inside arms loosely entwined—a detail Gary and I register simultaneously, an ether of intimacy encircling us like an embrace.

~

No guidebook, nor even personal testimony, can prepare one for the glad shock. A friend said simply he wished he could be there to catch me as I fell in a dead faint.

As the train slows to a halt, out the windows I see the standard parallel tracks, the standard chains of orange-red train cars at rest; a faded green one is pulling out. In the last mile, we *have* crossed water, which speeds my heart.

Yet out the windows, the unremarkable, unimaginative architecture of yet another train stop, this one half a century old, with massive sweeps of fascist concrete. We know we will be staying here four days, so we sit—on the outside calm, as if above the bustle, or as if we are old hands at this. Let the others gather their things in a frenzy and bump through the aisles and out the doors. This refusal to rush is Gary's influence, the rhythm of a painter who can spend months on a single twelve-by-fourteen-inch canvas.

At last our footsteps clack in the suddenly empty train car. Down the metal stair to the landing, then along the walkway as we shoulder our travel bags into the enormous hollow of the station proper. Glassed-in gift shops, snack counters, and currency exchange offices have taken bites from the open rectangle.

Today is mild. A low, woolly cloud mass, softening the edges of things, has hovered since we stepped from the apartment door in Bologna. Yet now, through the floor-to-ceiling windows and glass doors of the far wall, something about the light signals a change, a silvery cast, a burnish that draws us forward. We ignore an old man who thrusts small hotel ads into our hands; we stride toward the light, which leads to the broad stone terrace and stairs cascading to the Grand Canal of fifteenth-century Venice.

—the glow of not-quite-ochre walls, the glow of not-quite-peach; a row of four-story Renaissance houses, carved white wooden balcony posts, the crackling fragments of light along the water's surface, the *quiet*—Gary smiles and points toward both his ears; inside my head a refrain, *no cars, no cars*

—the drapery of three young men sprawled on the station stairs in bright white T-shirts and denim cutoffs, legs wide apart, the genitals of one peeking out; their heads thrown back and resting on their palms, staring at the clouds, all three with curly hair (one light, two dark) and features not yet edged by age, their loose-tied backpacks scattered on the steps—Gary nods; in my head, *the Graces, three Tadzios*

—the chug of the vaporetto motor in ripples up our legs, on our waterbus a density of bodies not stiff as in New York subway cars but a matter-of-fact, alongside-the-body community; heads turn this way and that, arms point—the radiance of church domes, the upsweep of palace balconies, and then on a crumbling dock, a couple necking; he sits, legs dangling above the water; she's on his lap, her legs looped around his back, her yellow skirt hiked up, a bottle of wine to their side on the weathered deck; on the vaporetto, a community of knowing, nodding heads

Sometimes naming the magic does not destroy it; sometimes naming calls the magic more directly forth. As we pull into the dock at the Piazza San Marco, I'm struck by the row of marble nudes arrayed atop the length of the Libreria Vecchia, their postures a compendium: adorations of the human form.

Climbing from the bobbing vaporetto to the landing, I

stumble—but don't. Gary, stepping up at my side, gazing toward the buzzing piazza, has looped his arm securely through mine.

ENVOI

We must make choices in Rome. Having spent our time awash in the iconography of religious paintings and frescoes from the Gothic period and the Renaissance, having spent our days in still, sometimes dark, places—the interiors of the churches and museums of Florence and Bologna and Venice—we decide on a change. We are ready for open space and the relative austerity of antiquity. If we haven't time for the Sistine Chapel and Vatican Museums, so be it.

Our first priority is the Roman Forum. As it happens, our hotel, chosen from a guidebook and secured by phone, is close to the Vatican. It's no trouble at all to pass through St. Peter's Square on our way to the ruins. The square, a great bowl formed by two semicircular colonnades, like arms extending from either side of the church, is so large, all that's human shrinks to unreality. Tourist buses, permitted to pull up on the edge of the square's cobbled skirt, look like Matchbox toys.

As Gary prepares to take a photo, three cardinals pop out from among the columns to our right. In their floor-length black robes, dusting the cobblestones, they seem like men on a conveyor belt, gliding, or men without bodies—only their heads and hands peek out from the heavy drapery, which swallows their trunks and limbs.

The cardinals aren't without color, however. Long tassels hang from brilliant pink sashes tied at their waists, and two wear skull-caps of the same neon color. This pink I think of as gay-pink, a shade several of my out-of-the-closet students wear proudly. One is never without some bit of the color, whether it be a large triangle silk-screened on a black T-shirt, or socks strobing from atop his Reeboks. Inspired by him, I purchased a bright pink visored cap for this trip—a perfect match for these men of the cloth.

With a flick of my hand, I signal to Gary I'm about to slip in with the clerics for a photo. My task is complicated, unfortunately, by the six carbine-toting guards who fan twenty feet back in a protective semicircle. I make my move (not too close), am not fired upon; Gary gets a snapshot; and we chuckle at this bit of Catholic color-irony—the church that would just as soon treat our kind like those bothersome Renaissance rationalists, some of whom were burned at the stake.

Even from a several-block distance, we can see we've made the right decision—the Roman Forum is a landscape of essentials, the ruins like giant bones scattered in an enormous garden. Behind the three forty-foot, fluted columns remaining of the Temple of the Castors, nothing but sky, an open and endless blue. The scale here is represented by implication: for the volume of a massive, stadium-size basilica, two and one-half arches of a single side wall; for a temple, a row of white marble nubs spaced five feet apart, like tooth stumps, where pillars once rose.

I must restrain myself from holding my arms outstretched, or from simply running. I welcome such openness, and the simplification of color: red (earth) and blue (sky) and white (marble) and brown (brick) and green (trees, grass). In the late June warmth, the urge is strong to simplify on bodily terms, to strip off our shirts and feel the sun on our skin as we walk our whole first day, and the morning of the second, in the Forum and on the hill above, the Palatine, the ruins of the rulers' palaces.

When the second afternoon turns cloudy, we head for the museums nearby to spend the last of our sight-seeing hours among the pre-Christian marble and bronze sculptures. In one room, nothing but heads, the busts of emperors and poets lined up on stepped rows. All particulars—an oblong skull, foreshortened brow, or twist of nose—faithfully conveyed: these are portraits. Elsewhere, along the walls and on pedestals in the rooms' centers, idealized studies of the human form, primarily male, figures from myth and pre-Christian religion: on Hercules and the Dying Gaul and Neptune, perfectly symmetrical pectorals, a precise line descending from the neck along the sternum, then branching in an arc to either side below the breasts and up to the smooth, hollowed pits of the arms; a fine crease running up the inside of each full thigh to the upper hip; calves and shoulders muscled, but modestly so, in balance; buttocks rounded and firm.

By accident, yet as if to focus our attention on the male body, we visit last the courtyard of the Palazzo dei Conservatori Museum. I grab hold of Gary's arm, gasping in amazed delight at sight of what is propped along the courtyard walls: enormous body parts. Something about the exaggeration makes me want to laugh. The scale is parody. Here, on a pedestal, a hand standing on its wrist, the forefinger pointing toward the sky, the whole of it six feet, end to end; nearby, an upper arm, perhaps ten feet long; at the back right corner, a head and neck the size of a tiny European sedan. These and the other fragments—feet, one elbow joint, a kneecap, a chunk of torso, and so on—were once unified in a towering statue of Constantine.

The clouds having lifted some, we decide we have just enough energy for a small detour on our walk to the hotel; we'll visit the Piazza Navona to see Bernini's Fountain of the Four Rivers. There are, in fact, three fountains on the square, each peopled by figures with rippling musculature—they've spent too long in the gym, by Golden Age standards. In something of a sight-seeing stupor, we have difficulty figuring which fountain is which. The one of Neptune, trident upraised, body twisted in combat with an octopus, is recognizable enough. But we must poke our noses into the guidebook's brief description twice to know which of the other two represents the rivers at the Earth's four corners.

A man approaches, shirt trailing from a back pocket, skin deeply tanned, a map of Rome in hand; we are kin, tourists in small ways lost. He asks directions to the Pantheon. Gary finds us on the map and helps the man, from England, chart a course. Off he heads. Briefly we turn to the fountains.

Breaking from the piazza's edge, we see the Brit two blocks ahead, crossing an empty street. His skin glows in the failing light— the ancients would approve, I think, of his balanced proportions. A sudden *bleat bleat* interrupts my thoughts; two tiny blue-and-white police cars, like mechanical bugs, skid to a halt, wedging our tourist brother in the street's painted median.

We quicken our step, close enough now to see a hand dart in and out of a police car window. A finger points to the shirt dangling from the man's butt, then to his chest. His brow crinkles in confusion, smooths—he tugs the shirt hastily over his head.

As the cops pull away, we lope to his side. "Don't go walking about without your top," he laughs. "I gather that in Rome, a shirtless man is something of an affront!"

A few blocks on, the sky, which seemed only moments before to have cleared, explodes. All along the street, pedestrians scurry to shelter under doorways. Under ours, a scooped, shell-shaped canvas awning, two young female shop clerks edge out to observe the spontaneous river rising toward the curb. People in clusters, who moments before idly window-shopped, or walked purposefully, as did we, toward their destinations, hug themselves against the surprising chill in the air. I see my face in theirs—I'm annoyed, I'm tired and cold, hands jammed in my pockets, rocking on the balls of my feet, eager for the comfort of our hotel room. Gary, who embraces rain anytime at our desert home for the sake of his garden vegetables and flowers, couldn't be more radiant.

And then we hear angels—four sweet, high voices, singing. I laugh, my body relaxes. Four teenage Gypsy girls skip down the middle of the river, holding hands in a line, kicking the water. Their long skirts fly, their dark hair shakes. In thin, short-sleeve cotton blouses, drenched to transparency, they light the street.

Reading the Body

Acknowledgments

My thanks to the editors of the following magazines and collections, in which some of the essays in this book first appeared or are forthcoming.

ENTRY POINTS, a college composition text and reader (Addison Wesley Longman, forthcoming): section 5 of "Manhood," under the title "Pass";

THE HARRINGTON GAY MEN'S FICTION QUARTERLY: "Care," "Chaos," "Ground," "Taboo," and "The Touch."

PUERTO DEL SOL: "Man Shrinking" (republished in *From Community to College*, a junior college composition textbook and reader: St. Martin's, 1996; and *The University Book*, a University of Arizona composition reader: Simon and Schuster, 1998);

WESTERN HUMANITIES REVIEW: "Permission";

WHISPERING CAMPAIGN: "Soldiers";

Over the years, many friends read versions of the essays in this book. Some offered thoughtful critical comments, which I did my best to live up to when revising; others, reading one or two essays at time, asked for more, offering what every writer needs most: pure encouragment. I'd like to thank Deb Jane Addis, Jim Allender, Beth Alvarado, Jean Binford, Patti Blanco, Roger Bowen, Karen Brennan, India Cooper, Barbara Cully, Alison Deming, Sandy Florence, Matt Gabrielson, Ruth Gardner, Hannah Glasston, Mike and Sue Hendershot, Raphael Kadushin, Robert Kaplan, Michael Marks, Maria Molina, Steve Orlen, Joan Sapinsley, Maribel Sosa, Kim Westerman, and last, especially, Susan Fox Rogers, the final reader, through whose faith, editorial insight, and personal agency the manuscript saw print.